BASIC MASONRY

By the Editors of Sunset Books

Sunset Books
VP, Sales & Marketing: Richard A. Smeby
Editorial Director: Bob Doyle
Production Director: Lory Day
Art Director: Vasken Guiragossian

Sunset Publishing Corporation
Chairman: Jim Nelson
President/CEO: Robin Wolaner
Chief Financial Officer: James E. Mitchell
Publisher, Sunset Magazine: Stephen J. Seabolt
Circulation Director: Robert L. Gursha
Editor, Sunset Magazine: William R. Marken

Basic Masonry was produced by
St. Remy Press
President: Pierre Léveillé
Managing Editor: Carolyn Jackson
Senior Editor: Heather Mills
Senior Art Director: Francine Lemieux
Art Director: Luc Germain
Assistant Editor: Rebecca Smollett
Designers: François Daxhelet, Hélène Dion,
    Jean-Guy Doiron, François Longpré
Picture Editor: Christopher Jackson
Contributing Illustrators: Michel Blais, Jacques Perrault
Production Manager: Michelle Turbide
System Coordinator: Eric Beaulieu
Photographer: Robert Chartier
Proofreaders: Jane Pavanel, Veronica Schami,
    Elizabeth Warwick
Indexer: Christine M. Jacobs
Administrator: Natalie Watanabe
Other Staff: Normand Boudreault, Lorraine Doré,
    Michel Giguère, Solange Laberge, Alfred LeMaitre

Book Consultants
Richard Day
Don Vandervort

Acknowledgments
Thanks to the following:
Association des manufacturiers de maçonnerie de beton,
    Montreal, Que.
Brick Institute of America, Reston, VA
Briqueterie St. Laurent, Laprairie, Que.
Centre Do-It D'Agostino, Montreal, Que.
Ducharme Quarry, Havelock, Que.
Matco-Ravary, St. Leonard, Que.
National Concrete Masonry Association, Herndon, VA
National Tile Contractors Association, Jackson, MS
Permacon Group Inc., Anjou, Que.
Portland Cement Association, Skokie, IL
Ramca Tiles Ltd., Montreal, Que.
RCP Block and Brick Company Inc.,
    Lemon Grove, CA
South Texas Stone Company, Houston, TX
Space Dimensions, Aylmer, Que.

Third printing May 1998

ISBN 0-376-01582-9
Library of Congress Catalog Card Number: 94-069964
Printed in the United States

CONTENTS

MASONRY MATERIALS

For the homeowner, building with masonry—brick, block, stone, tile, and concrete—has unique advantages. Masonry offers a combination of beauty, utility, ease of maintenance, and durability, since it is highly resistant to natural deterioration by wind, water, fire, sun, and pests. Indeed, the rough hand of human beings has proved the undoing of more masonry structures than has the relatively gentle hand of nature. Most surviving structures of the ancient world are of masonry, and the deterioration they show is due more often to warfare—and to succeeding generations' penchant for using them as a handy supply of building materials—than to their battles against the elements. The warm natural look of brick, tile, adobe, and stone has an earthy appeal. Even concrete, though it has a more modern look, is made of natural materials.

This book will guide you through the world of masonry and help you master the techniques necessary to build with these materials. The techniques are fairly easy to master. Starting on the next page, there is a catalog of masonry building materials, and—for inspiration—photographs of completed projects. Three how-to chapters follow: the first two give you step-by-step instructions for building walls and pavings from unit masonry—brick, concrete block, adobe, stone, and tile; the third deals with cast concrete. Finally, there is a chapter on the maintenance and repair of masonry.

Masonry work is work well rewarded. Properly built, your finished project can last almost as long as the earth from which it is made.

The colors and textures of masonry harmonize in this outdoor corner. A low brick retaining wall, brick-in-sand paving, and a higher, more rugged stone wall complement a tumble of flowers in this garden.

BRICK

Made of various clay mixtures, bricks once were molded by hand but now are usually extruded: The clay is forced through a die, then cut to size with wires. After drying, the bricks are fired in a kiln so that they become permanent; they can no longer be reduced to soft clay.

Bricks are used structurally in walls and pavings, both indoors and out. With the passage of time, their natural surface acquires a lovely patina, becoming more and more attractive. Brick is usually the material of choice for garden projects where appearance and upkeep are most important. A properly engineered brick wall needs little care; its life is measured in generations. Although brick has become relatively expensive, its cost can be justified when you consider its beauty, permanence, and maintenance-free character.

Bricks make an attractive veneer over homelier materials, such as concrete block, offering the advantage of brick's appearance with some of the strength, speed of installation, and economy of block work.

Bricks are small, so working with them is not taxing; on the other hand, the wall will rise rather slowly. Brick walls are mortared, and must be built on concrete foundations. A well-built brick wall is extremely strong in compression; that is, it resists crushing forces very well. It does not have much strength, though, in tension (stretching) and must be reinforced with steel wherever high tensile loads are expected—in structures such as high walls in windy or earthquake areas, or retaining walls.

For paving, the rough surface of common brick provides traction and reduces glare. The surface is porous, readily absorbing water. As the water evaporates, it cools the air and makes the surface cool underfoot. Unfortunately, it will just as readily absorb oil, grease, and paint—all of which may be hard to remove.

Types of brick surfaces vary from region to region; some of those available are shown at right. Each surface is likely to be found in various colors. See page 23 for information on brick sizes.

Steps to effective bricklaying begin on page 22; to pave with brick, turn to page 49.

A VARIETY OF BRICKS

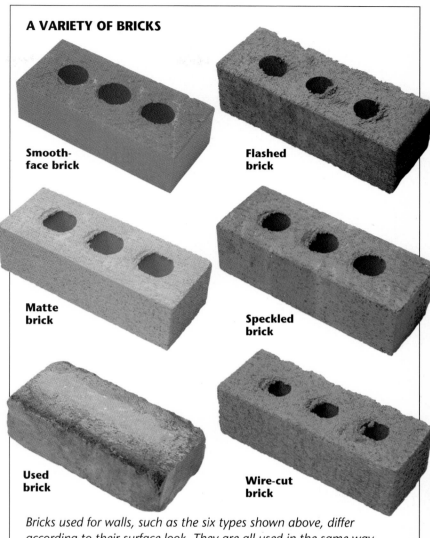

Smooth-face brick

Flashed brick

Matte brick

Speckled brick

Used brick

Wire-cut brick

Bricks used for walls, such as the six types shown above, differ according to their surface look. They are all used in the same way, except for used bricks, which are best used for appearance only, because their strength is unknown. However, new bricks, made to look used, are sometimes available.

Bricks used for purposes other than wall-building are shown below.

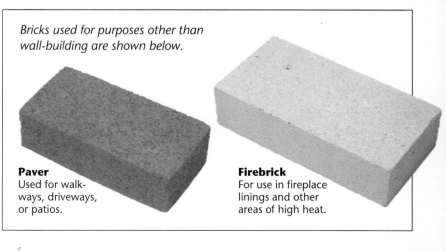

Paver
Used for walkways, driveways, or patios.

Firebrick
For use in fireplace linings and other areas of high heat.

A handsome combination of headers, soldiers, and stretchers (page 22), along with a carefully laid grille, gives this common-bond wall an uncommon look. Decorative pilasters reinforce the wall at the opening. Mortared borders retain the brick-in-sand walk. (Architects: Fisher-Friedman)

Bricks recycled from a patio torn up during remodeling get a new lease on life in an attractive driveway. These timeworn bricks are laid in mortar over a concrete slab.

Low steps, brick planters, and elaborate paving add up to a sophisticated and distinctive entry. (Architects: Sandy & Babcock)

BLOCK

Building and paving blocks can be made of concrete or adobe. Concrete block is less expensive than brick, making it your best choice for heavy-duty walls and for projects where costs must be kept down. Where appearance is important, you can choose from many decorative surfaces that catch the play of light, such as the slump or split-face blocks shown at right. Slump blocks go through a press that gives them an irregular appearance similar to trimmed stone or handmade adobe. Split-face blocks are broken apart in manufacture and resemble cut stone. Block can be veneered with brick, stone, or other material; it can also be sandblasted to reveal its aggregate, as well as painted, stuccoed, or plastered.

The large size of concrete blocks—8x8x16 inches is standard—makes for rapid progress in building. Most freestanding walls can be built with only one thickness of block. This is in marked contrast to brick, and it's a real timesaver that helps compensate for the blocks' rather cumbersome size and weight. Where extra strength is needed, the hollow cores can be filled easily with steel reinforcing rods and grout.

Concrete blocks are available in an array of sizes and shapes; all except slump blocks have precise dimensions, making it easy to plan and design your wall. Since the only factor limiting accuracy is your ability to maintain a consistent 3/8-inch mortar joint, working with concrete block can be quite exact—more so than with brick, where sizes may be slightly irregular.

Interlocking concrete pavers, developed in Europe, are increasingly popular in North America. They are made of extremely dense, pressure-formed concrete. Laid in sand with sanded joints, they form a surface more rigid than bricks. No paver can tip out of alignment without taking several of its neighbors with it; thus, the surface remains intact even under very heavy loads. Pavers are easy to lay and are generally about the same price as brick. A special variant, the turf-retaining block, is designed to carry lighter traffic while retaining and protecting ground-cover plants. See the chapter starting on page 49 for instructions on laying pavers.

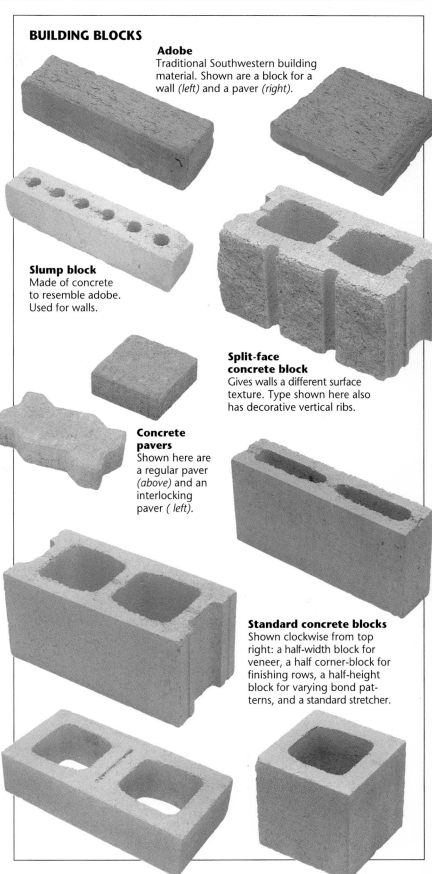

BUILDING BLOCKS

Adobe
Traditional Southwestern building material. Shown are a block for a wall (left) and a paver (right).

Slump block
Made of concrete to resemble adobe. Used for walls.

Split-face concrete block
Gives walls a different surface texture. Type shown here also has decorative vertical ribs.

Concrete pavers
Shown here are a regular paver (above) and an interlocking paver (left).

Standard concrete blocks
Shown clockwise from top right: a half-width block for veneer, a half corner-block for finishing rows, a half-height block for varying bond patterns, and a standard stretcher.

Adobe, the mud brick of the Southwest, is one of the world's oldest building materials. Modern adobe blocks are stabilized with portland cement or asphalt emulsions to make them impervious to water. Adobe adds character and a friendly, rustic charm, and is best used in open, generous gardens where the large size of the blocks will be in scale. The earth color of adobe looks good with natural woods and informal settings, but the blocks can be painted if you want a more formal feeling. Adobe is inexpensive unless it must be shipped long distances; then, costs may be high.

Because they weigh up to 45 pounds each, adobe blocks can be a chore to lay, so be sure to pace your work. A steel-reinforced concrete foundation helps prevent cracking due to soil shifting. Instructions for building with adobe begin on page 38.

Adobe pavers are available in square and rectangular shapes. Information on paving starts on page 49.

An adobe-like wall of white-painted slump blocks winds around a spa. The openings were created with half-size blocks. The expanse of exposed-aggregate paving is relieved by decorative strips of brick. (Landscape architects: Jones & Peterson)

Interlocking concrete pavers provide a decorative touch to these steps and walkway.

Adobe's natural, warm color contrasts with a splashy display of multicolored impatiens along this winding garden path. The blocks placed in the curved section were easy to cut and were laid on a bed of crushed rock.

Looking like stone, split-face concrete blocks form a retaining wall for this bark-covered play area. (Landscape architect: Ted Sutton)

STONE

Stone is labor-intensive—it takes a lot of time and effort to quarry, trim, haul, and store it. Even when found lying on the ground, it's a difficult material to handle and position. This didn't matter to the ancients; labor was cheap in those days. But now, stone is a luxury. Because of its expense (and also its lack of resistance to earthquakes), it is rarely used structurally and is reserved for applications where character and appearance are important.

For the garden, stone is never out of place. Both freestanding and retaining walls can be built either mortared or dry (unmortared). With dry walls, you can place plants in the crevices, blending the wall into the garden for a very pleasing effect.

Stonecraft can be difficult work; it is probably the most laborious of all the masonry techniques, requiring a strong back, a good eye, and lots of patience. Almost all forms of stone are denser, heavier, and larger than brick. Furthermore, the irregular shapes of all but the most exactly trimmed ashlar stones make it difficult to keep large walls plumb and true while maintaining good bonding. Working with stone also presents a demanding design challenge.

Stoneyards supply uncut (rubble) or cut (ashlar) stone of various types, some of which are shown at right. Cut stones are the more expensive. Synthetic stone veneers, made of cement mixtures, are often surprisingly like the real thing. You may want to consider them for their low cost and labor-saving qualities. Because of their light weight, there's usually no need to reinforce the structure they will cover.

Flagstone paving used to be more common than it is today, but still provides one of the toughest outdoor surfaces available. The subdued colors and irregular shapes greatly enhance most outdoor settings. River rock and fieldstone offer alternatives to the high cost of flagstone. These water-worn or glacier-ground stones produce a rustic, uneven paving that makes up in charm what it may lack in smoothness underfoot. You can also make your own "stones" out of concrete *(page 82)*.

THE NATURAL BEAUTY OF STONE

Roughly squared cobblestone
Suitable for both walls and paving. Granite shown here.

Rubble stone
Used for walls. Smoothly worn granite shown.

Slate
Often used for interior floors. Can range widely in color.

Flagstone
Makes elegant outdoor paving. Sandstone shown.

Imitation stone
Makes an inexpensive, light-weight veneer. Imitation granite river stone shown above left; imitation limestone, above right.

Ashlar stone
Used for walls; can be laid like brick. Sandstone shown.

A dry-laid rubble wall blooms with a profusion of colorful plants rooted in its earth-packed joints.

This sloping sandstone wall was laid more than 50 years ago. Ashlar work such as this is becoming increasingly rare; a search of older neighborhoods can turn up models for inspiration.

Natural river rock veneers a pool deck and retaining wall. Stones, mortared in place over concrete, ease the transition from plantings to pool. (Landscape architects: Singer & Hodges)

Synthetic stone veneer over a concrete-block planter and entry wall extends onto the house wall to muffle noise from a busy street—and the cost was less than half that of natural stone. The carefully fitted, ungrouted joints minimize exposed mortar. (Architect: Thomas Lile)

TILE

Tile is one of the oldest surfacing materials, found in ancient Egyptian and Roman homes and baths. Like brick, tile is a fired-clay product and it is available in a great variety of sizes and shapes; a sample of common types is shown at right.

Low-fired tile is porous and rather soft compared to high-fired tile such as porcelain, which is more vitreous (glasslike) and water-resistant. The composition of the clay and the heat of the firing make the difference. Both types are available either glazed or unglazed. A glaze is a thin, glassy coating bonded to the clay at very high temperatures in the kiln. Glaze adds and intensifies color, and gives the tile texture and durability.

Quarry tiles are extruded by squeezing the clay. They are available in natural clay colors and make a durable indoor or outdoor surface. Quarry tiles resist freezing and in cold climates are a good choice for outdoors.

Tile is equally well adapted to pavings and to wall coverings. In the kitchen or bathroom, it makes one of the most durable surfaces available for counters, walls, and floors. Extending a tile floor out onto a patio unites the spaces, or you can choose a contrasting color or surface for the outdoor area.

As an outdoor surface, tile can be as hard as the toughest stone, and like stone, it resists abrasion and soiling. It is more expensive than brick, but also more versatile. Most outdoor varieties are unglazed and take their color from the clay itself; they range from gray to brick color.

Even the finished surface of unglazed tile is likely to be slippery when wet, unless the tiles are quite rough. Tiles with special non-slip surfaces are available. Glazed tile can be used outdoors, but should be reserved for borders where people won't slip on it.

Tiles are commonly a foot square or less in size. They are also available in larger sizes and in a variety of other shapes, such as rectangles and hexagons. Still other shapes fit to create a pattern. Small colored tiles or handpainted tiles can be used as borders or to vary the pattern.

This book will concentrate on the use of tile for outdoor paving; instructions are found beginning on page 49.

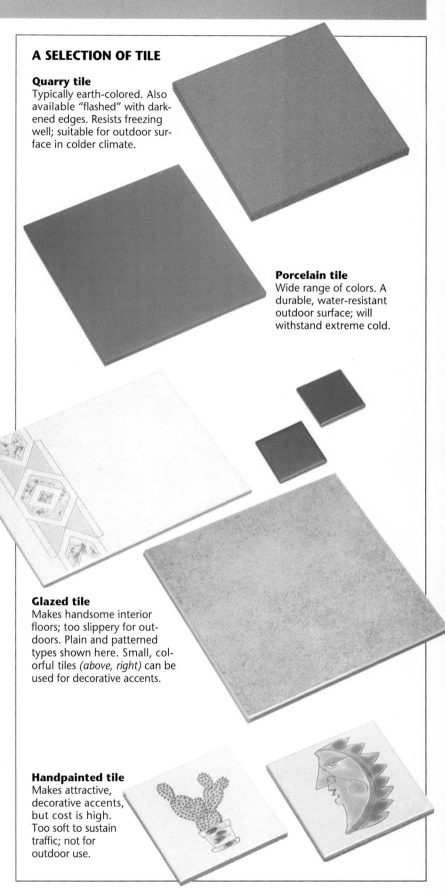

A SELECTION OF TILE

Quarry tile
Typically earth-colored. Also available "flashed" with darkened edges. Resists freezing well; suitable for outdoor surface in colder climate.

Porcelain tile
Wide range of colors. A durable, water-resistant outdoor surface; will withstand extreme cold.

Glazed tile
Makes handsome interior floors; too slippery for outdoors. Plain and patterned types shown here. Small, colorful tiles (above, right) can be used for decorative accents.

Handpainted tile
Makes attractive, decorative accents, but cost is high. Too soft to sustain traffic; not for outdoor use.

Mexican floor tiles make a beautiful and practical surface. Here, they're accented by kitchen counters of hand-painted tile, and matching window trim. The wine rack, too, is tile—unglazed tile drainpipe. (Architect: Alfred T. Gilman. Designer: Windom Hawkins)

Sand-colored quarry tiles transform plain concrete slabs into an inviting entry. Each square tile is surrounded by lozenge-shaped "pickets" to create an octagonal pattern. (Design: Designed Environ, Inc.)

CAST CONCRETE

Concrete is a mixture of portland cement, sand, aggregate (usually stone or gravel), and water. Cement is the "glue" that binds everything together and gives the finished product its hardness and durability. The sand and aggregate act as fillers and help control shrinkage. Once concrete hardens, it forms a dense, permanent material with enormous compressive strength. The use of steel reinforcement strengthens the material against tension as well, making possible everything from your home's foundation to sweeping freeway ramps and graceful bridges.

Cast concrete can be complicated to work with—a patio or a low concrete wall will probably involve more planning and preparation time than time spent actually placing and finishing the concrete. A form needs to be built and mounted, and concrete must be mixed. For the do-it-yourselfer, concrete is a logical choice for pavings, garden pools, and other small projects. This book covers only basic cast concrete work—footings and slabs; see page 62 for instructions. You will need to build concrete footings for most of the kinds of walls shown in the next chapter. You may also want to use concrete for edgings when paving with unit masonry (page 52).

You will often hear the term "poured concrete." In fact this term is misleading because concrete should never be watered down so much that it can be poured—concrete this thin is likely to crack or crumble later. In this book, we will use the terms "cast" and "placing" instead of "poured" and "pouring," respectively. Similarly, we use the term "plastic," not "wet," for fresh mortar that hasn't set.

The appearance of cast concrete is limited only by your ingenuity. Some of the possibilities are shown at right.

THE DIFFERENT FACES OF CONCRETE

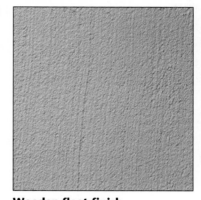

Wooden float finish
Float leaves a semi-smooth texture that is still rough enough to be glare-free and slip-resistant.

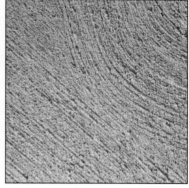

Broomed surface
Best where maximum traction is needed. Straight and wavy patterns are easy to produce.

Steel trowel finish
Trowel smooths concrete to a dense reflective surface suitable for enclosed patios and interiors. This slab was tinted brown.

Travertine finish
Produced when mortar is dashed onto newly placed concrete; troweling produces a stony layered look. Here both concrete and mortar have been tinted to bring out texture.

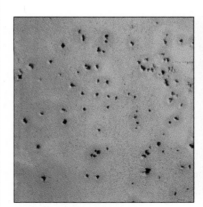

Rock salt surface
Salt is embedded while concrete is soft; salt is later washed out, leaving the pockmarks.

Exposed-aggregate surface
Used for both safety and attractiveness. Selected aggregate is embedded after concrete is placed, then exposed with hose and broom.

A low concrete wall provides safety, yet doesn't obscure this magnificent view. The tinted pool deck has a rock salt finish. (Landscape architects: Singer & Hodges)

Variety in color and texture is provided by cast-concrete steps with railroad-tie headers. The ties were used as forms for the concrete; left in place, they also make a functional edge. Pressure-treated peeler logs border the steps. (Landscape architect: William Louis Kapranos)

Large concrete stepping-stones seeded with smooth aggregate and variegated pebbles make a handsome entry. The spaces between the stones invite the growth of ground cover, softening the edges. (Designer: Carolyn Susmann)

WALLS: BRICK, BLOCK, ADOBE, AND STONE

Masonry is your best choice when you want a wall that will last—one that you can build, and then forget. In this chapter you'll find step-by-step instructions on how to build walls of brick, concrete block, adobe, and stone. The instructions apply equally to such projects as planters, borders, steps, hearths, and barbecues—once you've mastered the basic techniques needed to build walls with each material, you'll be able to strike off on your own.

These materials are examples of what is called unit masonry; that is, masonry materials that are made in units small enough for one person to handle. (A chapter on continuous masonry—cast concrete—begins on page 62.) For help in choosing a material for your project, see the materials chapter.

Unit masonry materials are generally assembled using mortar. A discussion of mortar—what it is, how to mix and how to use it—starts on page 20 and is followed by subsections on how to handle each material.

Shown here is a course of headers being laid over a course of stretchers to create a "common bond" brick wall. This is one of the many types of walls you'll learn to build in this chapter.

BEFORE YOU BEGIN

Before finalizing plans for your wall, drop by your local building department and inquire about regulations that may apply to your project. These will specify how close to your property line you can build, how high you can build, what kind of foundation you'll need, whether or not the wall will require steel reinforcing, whether inspections will be necessary, and more.

For some, the mere thought of trekking down to the building department in order to dive into a mass of red tape is intimidating. In reality, the building department can be a real asset to any do-it-yourselfer. Building officials are usually pleased to help you with your project, and they can be of great assistance in steering you in the right direction. Their job is to enforce the building code, which is the set of regulations that specifies minimum standards for materials and workmanship. Constructing your wall—or any project—to these standards is cheap insurance; following the code will help assure you of the structural integrity of whatever you build.

In the past, building departments were not especially concerned with non-load-bearing walls (walls that carry only their own weight), but in this era of litigation, things have changed. Many municipalities now require a building permit for masonry walls over 3 feet high; some, especially in earthquake areas, may also require that the wall either conform to their standard design or be certified by an engineer before a permit is granted. Be sure to check. Walls lower than 3 feet and other small-scale projects will probably not require a permit, but some building departments will agree to look at a sketch anyway.

The how-to instructions that follow refer to walls less than 3 feet high, and the discussions of steel reinforcing are intended only as introductions. If your project is 3 feet high or more, or if you need steel reinforcing, be sure to consult your building department.

Many tasks involved in masonry work require the basic safety gear shown below. Dry portland cement is irritating to the eyes, nose, and mouth; wear a dust mask and goggles when working with it. Wet mortar and concrete are caustic to the skin; wear gloves and tuck your sleeves into them. If you do come into contact with wet mortar or concrete, flush your skin with water. Always bend your knees, not your back, when lifting heavy units such as adobe and stone.

You may want to invest in some of the specialized tools shown opposite. Some of them, such as the story pole, batter gauge, and strikeoff, must be built to suit the job. Others can be improvised; for example, an ordinary level used against a straight 2x4 can substitute for the extra-long mason's level. You will also need a number of tools that you are likely to have in your workshop or garden shed—brushes, shovels, a wheelbarrow, a small sledgehammer, a rubber mallet, and a carpenter's square. In fact, all you may need to buy are a good trowel and brick set.

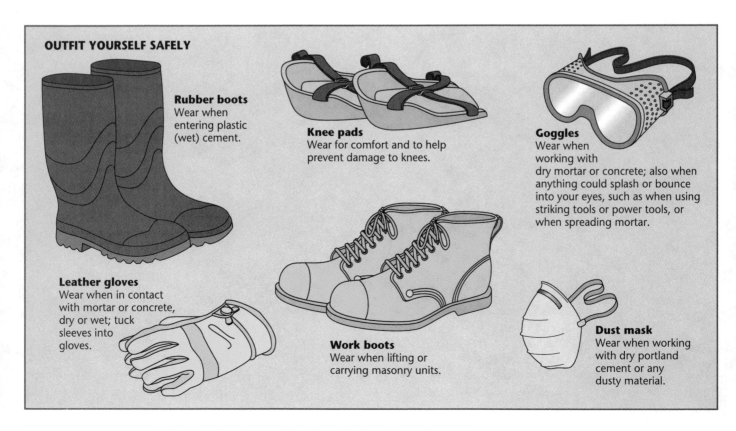

OUTFIT YOURSELF SAFELY

Rubber boots
Wear when entering plastic (wet) cement.

Knee pads
Wear for comfort and to help prevent damage to knees.

Goggles
Wear when working with dry mortar or concrete; also when anything could splash or bounce into your eyes, such as when using striking tools or power tools, or when spreading mortar.

Leather gloves
Wear when in contact with mortar or concrete, dry or wet; tuck sleeves into gloves.

Work boots
Wear when lifting or carrying masonry units.

Dust mask
Wear when working with dry portland cement or any dusty material.

TOOLS OF THE TRADE: UNIT MASONRY

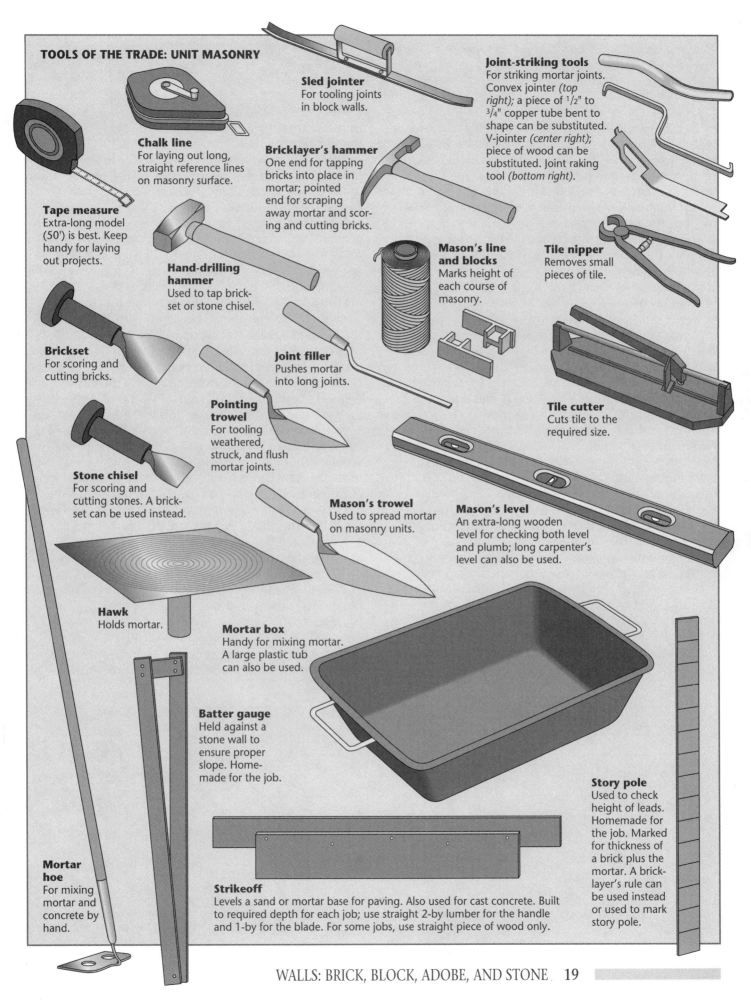

Chalk line
For laying out long, straight reference lines on masonry surface.

Sled jointer
For tooling joints in block walls.

Joint-striking tools
For striking mortar joints. Convex jointer *(top right);* a piece of ¹/₂" to ³/₄" copper tube bent to shape can be substituted. V-jointer *(center right);* piece of wood can be substituted. Joint raking tool *(bottom right).*

Tape measure
Extra-long model (50') is best. Keep handy for laying out projects.

Bricklayer's hammer
One end for tapping bricks into place in mortar; pointed end for scraping away mortar and scoring and cutting bricks.

Hand-drilling hammer
Used to tap brickset or stone chisel.

Mason's line and blocks
Marks height of each course of masonry.

Tile nipper
Removes small pieces of tile.

Brickset
For scoring and cutting bricks.

Joint filler
Pushes mortar into long joints.

Tile cutter
Cuts tile to the required size.

Pointing trowel
For tooling weathered, struck, and flush mortar joints.

Stone chisel
For scoring and cutting stones. A brickset can be used instead.

Mason's trowel
Used to spread mortar on masonry units.

Mason's level
An extra-long wooden level for checking both level and plumb; long carpenter's level can also be used.

Hawk
Holds mortar.

Mortar box
Handy for mixing mortar. A large plastic tub can also be used.

Batter gauge
Held against a stone wall to ensure proper slope. Homemade for the job.

Story pole
Used to check height of leads. Homemade for the job. Marked for thickness of a brick plus the mortar. A bricklayer's rule can be used instead or used to mark story pole.

Mortar hoe
For mixing mortar and concrete by hand.

Strikeoff
Levels a sand or mortar base for paving. Also used for cast concrete. Built to required depth for each job; use straight 2-by lumber for the handle and 1-by for the blade. For some jobs, use straight piece of wood only.

MIXING AND APPLYING MORTAR

Mortar is the "glue" that binds masonry units together. Beyond this, it has several other functions: It seals out wind and water, compensates for variations in the size of masonry units, anchors metal ties and reinforcements, and provides various decorative effects, depending on how the joints are tooled, or "struck."

Ingredients: Mortar recipes vary according to their use, but the ingredients are always the same: portland cement, sand, lime, and water. (Mortar for paving is made without lime.) Consult your building supplier about the quantity of mortar you'll need. For general purposes, you should use Type I or Type II **portland cement**; it is widely available. Although **lime** weakens mortar somewhat, it is vital for making the mix workable. **Hydrated lime**, used in mortar, is caustic, and you should take care to avoid contact with your skin. Instead of using lime to make mortar, a simpler method uses masonry cement, which already contains lime. Buy Type II masonry cement. (Do not use masonry cement for making concrete.) **Mortar sand** should be clean, sharp-edged, and free of impurities such as salt, clay, dust, and organic matter. Never use beach sand—its grains are too rounded. Particle size should range evenly from about 1/8 inch to fine. Use drinkable **water** for mortar; never salt water or water high in acid or alkali content.

Grout is concrete that is thin enough to pour. It's used to fill cavities in masonry walls, such as the cells of concrete blocks *(page 37)* or the space between the wythes of a brick wall *(page 24)*. When grout sets up it locks a wall together into an essentially monolithic structure. Steel reinforcing is always secured in a wall by grouting. To make grout, make a concrete mix as described on page 64 using concrete sand and, if you wish, pea gravel to fill out the mixture cheaply; add water so that the grout is just liquid enough to pour.

Measuring: The most accurate way to proportion ingredients is to weigh them, but because this is rarely practical, masons usually go by volume. Specific recipes for various types of mortar are given in the chart below. Once you're ready to begin, you'll probably find it more convenient to measure out your ingredients by the bag, bucket, or shovelful. The key is to be consistent in measuring so that your mortar will be the same from batch to batch. Since mortar must be mixed in fairly small batches—large batches tend to harden before they're used up—masons often mix by the shovelful.

Mortar does become weaker as its lime and sand content go up, but it also becomes cheaper because the amount of cement (the most expensive ingredient) goes down in proportion. Type S mortar offers a good medium of strength and workability and can be used both above and below ground. Type N mortar should be used above ground. If your job is small, prepackaged mortar, sold by the bag at building supply stores, is your best bet—the extra cost is usually offset by the convenience of not having to purchase and measure separate ingredients. Although brand recipes vary, most manufacturers produce a mortar similar to Type N. If you buy Type N, you can add about 4 cups portland cement to a 60-pound sack to approximate Type S.

Mixing: In mixing mortar, the dry ingredients are first measured out and mixed, either in a power mixer or by hand *(opposite)*, then the water is added and mixed in. The amount of water cannot be specified in advance, as it depends entirely upon the composition of the mortar and the absorption rate of the masonry units to be laid, factors that can vary according to the weather.

Ready for use, your mortar should have a smooth, uniform, buttery consistency; it should spread well and stick to vertical surfaces, yet not smear the face of

MORTAR FORMULAS (By parts)		Type	Portland cement	Hydrated lime	Masonry cement	Masonry sand	Chief characteristic
Cement-lime mortars		M	1/4	1/4	—	3	High compressive strength
		N	1	1	—	6	More workable
		S	1	1/2	—	4 1/2	Best blend of workability and strength
Masonry cement mortars		M	1	—	1	6	High compressive strength
		N	—	—	1	3	More workable
		S	1/2	—	1	4 1/2	Best blend of workability and strength

your work. Add water a little at a time and mix until these requirements have been met.

Applying mortar: A master mason at work is a study in skill, speed, and concentration. If you can, try to observe one; you'll find the time well rewarded. To lay masonry units, you need to develop certain skills with the trowel, as shown below. If throwing a line turns out to be too difficult, you can cut off narrower slices of mortar and lay them down one trowel at a time.

Tempering: Keep your mortar workable, or "well tempered," by sprinkling a little water as necessary and remixing. However, don't expect mortar more than a couple of hours old to revive sufficiently for use; discard it and mix a smaller batch next time.

Curing: Curing mortar ensures that the cement and water combine chemically as the mortar hardens. To cure mortar joints, keep them moist for four days by spraying them periodically.

Mixing mortar

TOOLKIT
- Power mixer, or wheelbarrow or mortar box and mortar hoe, or walk-along mixer
- Square shovel

Using a power mixer
For large jobs, power mixers can be rented in a variety of sizes. With the mixer running, add some water, half the sand, and all of the lime. CAUTION: Never put the shovel inside the mixer. Next, add all of the cement, the rest of the sand, and enough water to achieve the right consistency. The mixer should run for at least 3 or 4 minutes once all the water is added. Mix only enough to last you about 2 hours; more than that is likely to be wasted.

Mixing by hand
Small amounts of mortar can readily be mixed by hand. You'll need a wheelbarrow or a mortar box, and a hoe. Mix the sand, cement, and lime well before adding water. Hoe the dry ingredients into a pile, make a hole in the top, and add some water; mix, then repeat as often as necessary to achieve the proper consistency.

Another option is the "walk-along" mixer, which effectively streamlines the hand-mixing procedure. In essence, it is like a power mixer—the difference is that you are the motor. Load in the ingredients as for a power mixer, walking the mixer along to blend them. You'll need to be able to do this close to your worksite since the loaded mixer is quite heavy; be sure there are no intervening flights of stairs.

Applying mortar

TOOLKIT
- Mason's trowel
- Sheet of 1/2" plywood, 2' square, to use as a mortar board

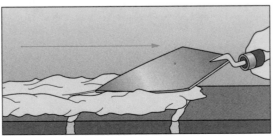

Throwing a mortar line and buttering
To load your trowel, place one or two shovelfuls of mortar on a wet mortar board. Slice off a wedge and scoop it up (an 8" or 10" trowel holds the right amount for brickwork). Give the trowel a shake to dislodge the excess.

To throw a line, bring your arm back toward your body and rotate the trowel, depositing the mortar in an even line about 1" thick, one brick wide, and 3 stretchers long *(left, top and middle)*, or the width of 3 headers if you're laying headers. Practice on the mortar board until you get the knack. Once the line is thrown, furrow it with the point of the trowel *(left, bottom)*. Divide the mortar; don't scrape it toward you. The furrow ensures that the bricks are bedded evenly and that excess mortar is squeezed out to either side as the bricks are laid

Buttering—a self-descriptive term—is used to apply mortar to the ends of masonry units. Load a small amount of mortar onto the end of the trowel and spread it on the brick. Mortar consistency is the key to buttering; it should be stiff enough not to drip, yet wet enough to stick.

BUILDING A BRICK WALL

Building with brick is pleasant work. The units are sized for easy one-handed lifting, and bricklaying takes on a certain rhythm once you get the hang of it. As with all building projects, planning and attention to detail are the keys.

This section guides you through the design and construction of a freestanding garden wall—your best introduction to bricklaying. We start with instructions for a straight wall; corner treatments are explained starting on page 28. Finally, we show you how to "strike" the joints. High walls (over 2 or 3 feet) require reinforcing, and long walls (over 60 feet) need a control joint; check your local codes.

Bricks can be oriented in different ways, with each orientation having a special term, as illustrated at right. Combining these orientations creates different bond patterns *(below)*. The instructions in this section are for building a common bond wall.

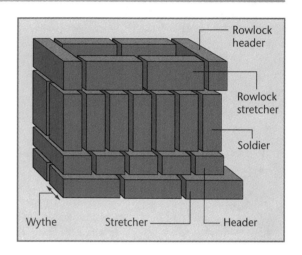

Rowlock header

Rowlock stretcher

Soldier

Header

Wythe   Stretcher

Designing a footing for a brick wall

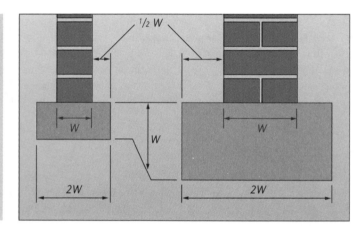

¹/₂ W

W

W

W

2W

2W

Building the footing

Concrete is the best material for footings. Codes usually specify a footing as deep as the width of the wall (W) and twice as wide (2W), with the wall centered above *(left)*. Complete instructions for building a concrete footing can be found on page 67. Always be sure to check your local building codes before proceeding.

Designing a wall

Choosing a bond pattern

Over the years, masons have developed patterns for laying bricks. Be sure to check with your building department before making a final decision on a bond pattern; if your wall requires steel reinforcing, some bonds may be more adaptable than others. See pages 28 to 31 for corner treatments.

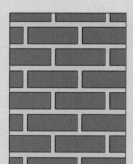

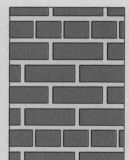

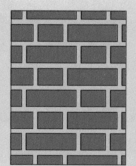

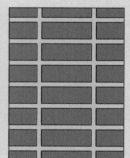

Running bond
Easy to lay. Mainly used for veneers and single-thickness partitions. Double thicknesses must be linked with metal ties.

Common bond
Also referred to as "American bond." Has headers every fifth course; strong and easy to lay.

Flemish bond
Alternates headers and stretchers in each course. Both decorative and structural.

English bond
Alternate courses of headers and stretchers. Forms very strong walls. Requires cutting bricks at corners.

Stack bond
Usually used for decorative effect in veneers. Weak; must be liberally reinforced if it is to be used structurally.

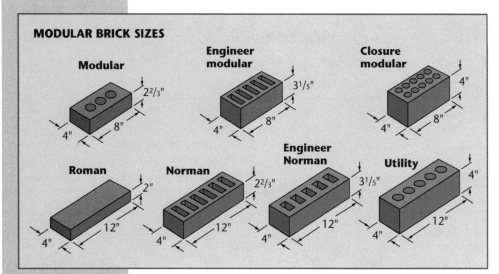

MODULAR BRICK SIZES

Modular
2²/₃"
8"
4"

Engineer modular
3¹/₅"
4" 8"

Closure modular
4"
8"
4"

Roman
2"
12"
4"

Norman
2²/₃"
12"
4"

Engineer Norman
3¹/₅"
12"
4"

Utility
4"
12"
4"

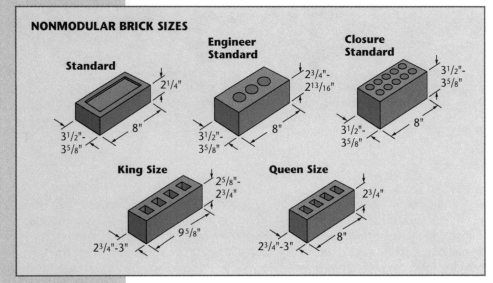

NONMODULAR BRICK SIZES

Standard
2¹/₄"
8"
3¹/₂"–3⁵/₈"

Engineer Standard
2³/₄"–2¹³/₁₆"
8"
3¹/₂"–3⁵/₈"

Closure Standard
3¹/₂"–3⁵/₈"
8"
3¹/₂"–3⁵/₈"

King Size
2⁵/₈"–2³/₄"
9⁵/₈"
2³/₄"–3"

Queen Size
2³/₄"
8"
2³/₄"–3"

Illustration courtesy of the Brick Institute of America

Choosing brick size

Many bricks are made in modular size—the three dimensions divide evenly into each other. The standard modular brick measures 2²/₃"x4"x8", so that two headers or three rowlocks will equal a stretcher. Those dimensions are nominal; they include the width of a standard ¹/₂" mortar joint, and actual dimensions of the standard brick are reduced accordingly. Nonmodular bricks are sold by their actual size. It is common for bricks to vary somewhat from specified dimensions. To calculate the quantity of bricks you'll need for your project, consult your building supplier.

Other sizes of modular and nonmodular bricks may also be available. Only the names Standard, Roman, and Norman are used throughout the industry. Names of other sizes may vary, so it's best to ask for bricks by size. The names shown in the illustrations are those used by the Brick Institute of America.

Reinforcing long, low walls

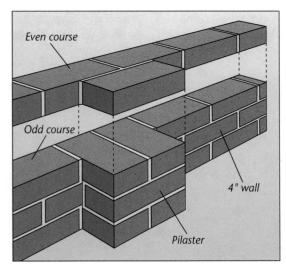

Even course

Odd course

4" wall

Pilaster

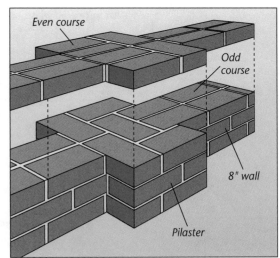

Even course

Odd course

8" wall

Pilaster

Building pilasters

Reinforce long walls every 12' with pilasters. They are locked into the wall by overlapping the bricks in alternate courses as shown for a single-wythe wall *(above, left)* or a double-wythe wall *(above, right)*.

REINFORCING RUNNING BOND

A simple way to add steel reinforcing to a wall built in running bond is to pour grout—thin, soupy concrete *(page 20)*—between the two wythes. Insert steel rods, called reinforcing rods, or "rebars," into the grout right down to the footing, once it has stiffened slightly. Or, place bars in the footing when it is poured, build around them and grout *(below, left)*.

Special steel ties of various patterns are made for reinforcing brick masonry. Two of the most common, Z-bar and metal ties, are shown below right.

Exact specifications and techniques for steel reinforcing are detailed in building codes; for further information consult your building department.

STEEL REINFORCING

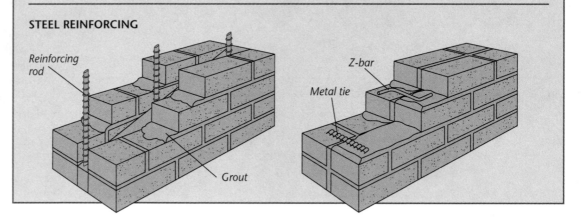

Reinforcing rod

Grout

Z-bar

Metal tie

Putting up a brick wall (common bond)

TOOLKIT
- Chalk line
- Mason's trowel
- Ruler, tape measure, or story pole
- Mason's line

1 Preparing to work
Careful location of the site will contribute to your wall's longevity. Choose a place where drainage is good and the soil is firm. Avoid locating the wall near the root systems of large trees; the growing roots can exert a nearly irresistible pressure and may crack your footing. Consult local codes for possible legal restrictions on the location of your project. Turn to page 67 for information on constructing the footing. You can begin laying the bricks after the footing has cured about two days. Distribute your bricks along the site in stacks. This will save time and help develop a rhythm to your bricklaying. Unless they are already damp, hose them down several hours before you begin to prevent them from absorbing too much moisture from the mortar. Save any broken bricks for cutting. Have a hose or bucket of water handy for rinsing your trowel and other tools as you work and also for keeping your mortar well tempered *(page 21)*.

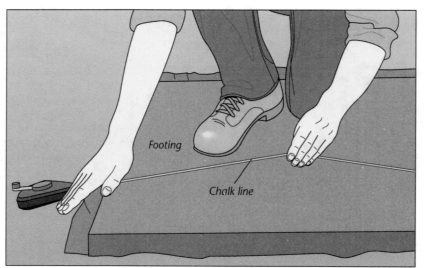

Footing

Chalk line

2 Marking the footing
Locate the outer edge of the wall by measuring in from the edge of the footing at each end so that the wall is centered. Stretch a chalk line between the two points and snap it to mark your guideline.

3 ▶ Laying a dry course

Lay a single course of stretcher bricks out along your chalk line the full length of the wall in order to mark the brick spacing on the footing. Allow 1/2" spaces for the head joints, marking them on the foundation with a pencil as you go. If possible, adjust the head joint width to allow you to lay the course without cutting any bricks.

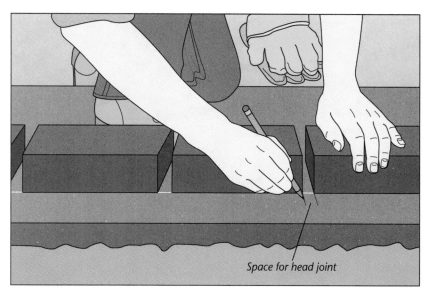

Space for head joint

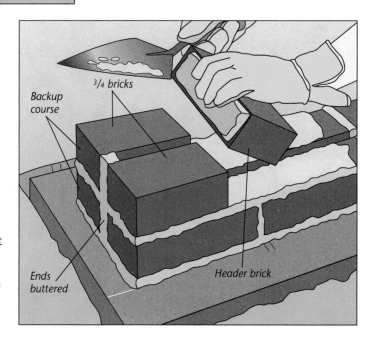

Pencil marks

4 ◀ Laying the first bricks

Take up bricks from the dry course. Throw a mortar line *(page 21)* three bricks long, leaving the markings, and lay the first three bricks. Butter the head-joint ends of the second and third bricks and place them with a shoving motion so that the mortar is squeezed out of all sides of the joint. Use a ruler, tape measure, or story pole to check the course for correct height, then carefully check that bricks are plumb and level, using your trowel handle to tap them into place. Never pull on a brick, as this breaks the bond. Check the head-joint thickness against your pencil marks and trim off any excess mortar.

5 ▶ Beginning the backup and header courses

Lay three backup bricks just as you did the first three. Use your level to check that the courses are at the same height in each wythe, and use a header brick to check the overall width of the wall. Butter enough of the inside edge of the first backup brick to seal the end of the two wythes, as shown. Otherwise, do not mortar the two wythes together.

Cut two 3/4 bricks to begin the header course, again buttering a bit of the inside edge of the backup brick; then lay three header bricks.

Backup course

3/4 bricks

Ends buttered

Header brick

HOW DO I CUT A BRICK?

If you want really precise brickwork, or are using extra-hard bricks such as "clinkers," you'll need to rent a masonry saw or purchase a special blade for your circular saw. Softer bricks are easy to cut without a saw: Wearing safety goggles, score the brick, placed on sand or earth, by tapping a brickset with a hand-drilling hammer. Go all around the brick, then cut with a sharp blow to the brickset.

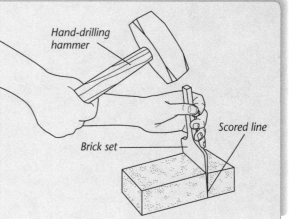

Hand-drilling hammer

Scored line

Brick set

---

6 ▶ **Finishing the lead**
Continue laying stretchers until the lead is five courses high, as shown. (Note that the fourth course begins with a single header.) Use your level as a straightedge to check that the lead is true on each of its surfaces *(right)*. Now go to the other end of the footing and build another lead, following steps 4 to 6.

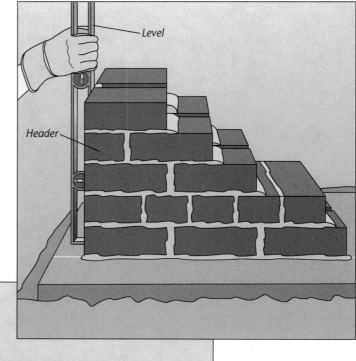

Level

Header

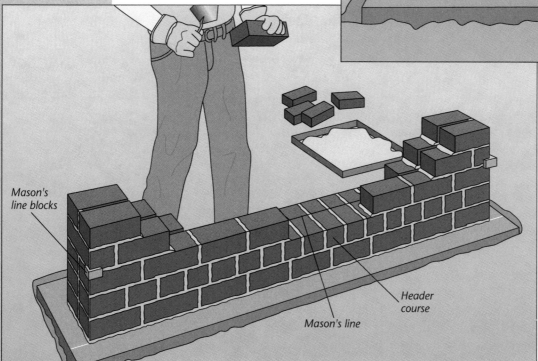

Mason's line blocks

Mason's line

Header course

7 ◀ **Filling in**
Stretch a mason's line between the completed leads as shown; then, begin laying the outer course. Keep the line about 1/16" away from the bricks and flush with their top edges; double-check the bricks with a ruler or story pole, since the line will sag if the wall is long. Lay bricks from both ends toward the middle.

Closer brick

Mason's line

8 Building to the top of the leads

Butter the ends of the last gap, then butter the last, or closer, brick on both ends and insert it straight down as shown. (You may have to trim this brick to make it fit.) Mortar should be squeezed from the joints. Continue laying the outer courses until you reach the top of the leads. Then, shift the mason's line to the back of the wall and begin laying the backup courses. Always use the mason's line, level, and ruler or story pole to check the accuracy of your work.

9 Going higher

To continue upward, build new five-course leads at each end of the wall, repeating steps 4-8. Keep a constant check on your work as you go, with a level, and ruler and story pole. Sight down the wall periodically to make sure it's true.

10 Planning the cap

You can cap your wall in many ways, but the simplest is a row of header bricks on edge—called rowlocks. Lay them out dry as shown, allowing for mortar joints. If the last brick overlaps the end of the wall, mark it at the point of overlap. Score and cut this brick *(page 26)* on the line you've marked.

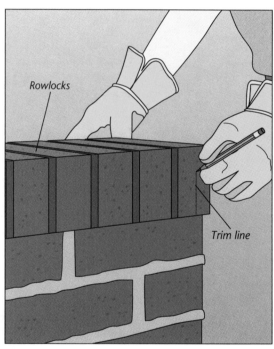

Rowlocks

Trim line

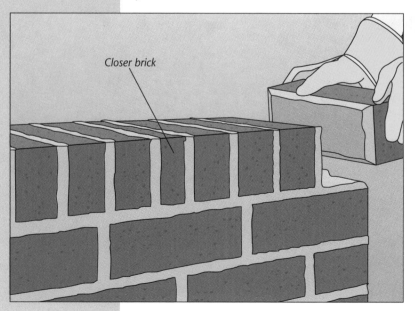

Closer brick

11 Laying the cap bricks

Throw mortar lines and begin laying the cap. Each succeeding brick should be well buttered on its face, and you should keep a careful check on joint thickness as you go.

If you have cut a brick, "bury" it four or five bricks from the end *(left)*, where it will be less noticeable. When you have laid the last brick, go over your work carefully with a level, checking the cap for alignment in all directions.

TOOLKIT
• Chalk line
• Tape measure
• Level
• Carpenter's square
• Mortar board
• Mason's trowel
• Soft-headed steel hammer
• Brickset

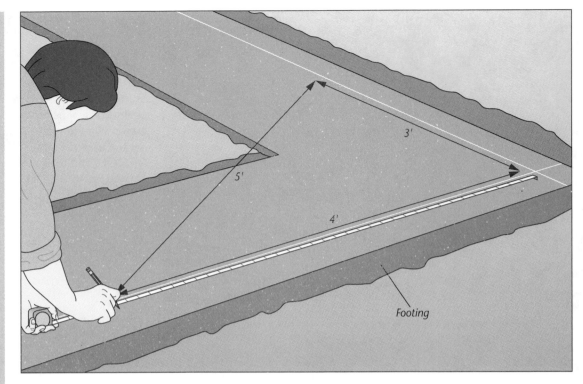

Footing

1 Laying out the corners
First snap chalk lines. Then check that they are absolutely square by using the 3-4-5 rule: Measure 3' along one line and 4' along the other. Now measure the distance between these two points. It should be 5'; if it isn't, adjust your lines. Using larger multiples of 3, 4, and 5—such as 6-8-10—will assure even greater accuracy.

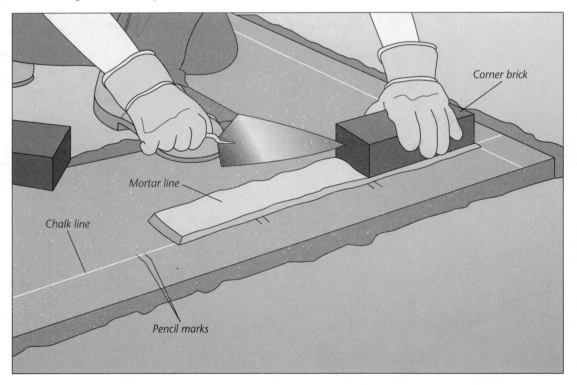

Corner brick

Mortar line

Chalk line

Pencil marks

2 Starting the corner lead
After making a dry run for the entire wall (*page 25, step 3*), lay the first brick exactly at the corner, lining it up carefully with your chalk lines.

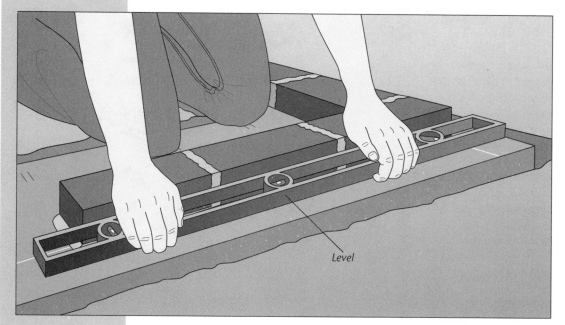

3 Tailing out the lead

Lay the remaining four lead bricks, checking carefully for accuracy. Masons call this "tailing out" the lead. Use a level to check level and plumb, as well as the bricks' alignment, as shown. A carpenter's square will also help.

Level

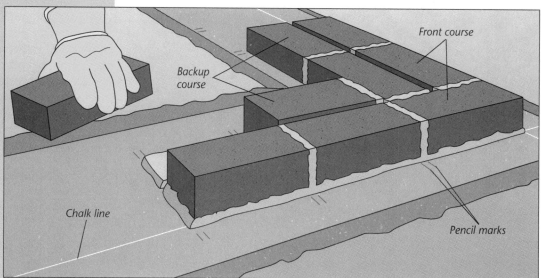

4 Laying the backup course

Throw mortar lines and lay the backup course as shown. Make sure not to disturb the front course, and remember that there is no mortar joint between these courses. Be sure that the backup course is level with the first one.

Front course

Backup course

Chalk line

Pencil marks

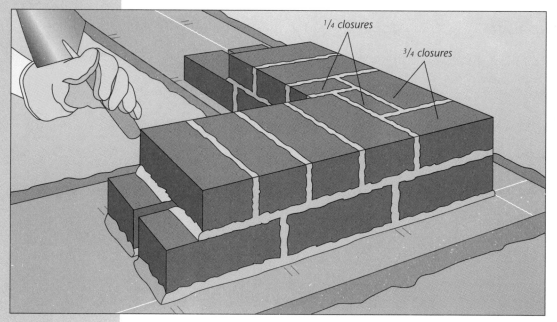

5 Starting the header course

Take two bricks and cut them into ³/₄ and ¹/₄ pieces. These are known in the building trade as "closures." Lay them as shown and complete the lead header course.

¹/₄ closures

³/₄ closures

6 ▶ Completing the lead

Now lay the leads for the next three stretcher courses. Note that each of these courses is the same as the first course, except the fourth course, which begins with a header. Check your completed lead for accuracy, and repeat these steps for the other corners in the wall. Now you're ready to finish the wall between leads, as shown on pages 26 to 27.

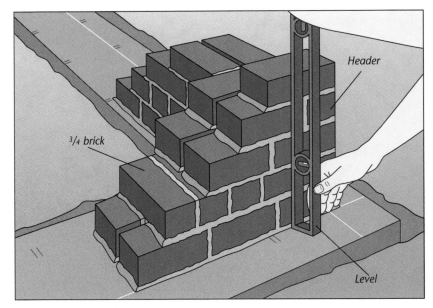

Header

³/₄ brick

Level

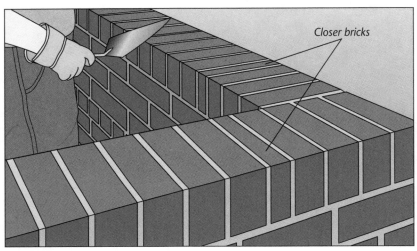

Closer bricks

7 ▶ Topping off the corner

Plan and lay the rowlock cap as shown on page 27. Note that the cap course starts flush with one edge of the corner: Lay these bricks first, and then start the other leg of the corner by butting the bricks against the first ones. Use closer bricks as needed *(page 27)*.

ASK A PRO

WHAT OTHER KIND OF WALL CAN I BUILD?

Serpentine walls were used by Thomas Jefferson in his architectural designs 200 years ago, and they are still popular today. The distinctive, sinuous curve of the wall is actually an engineering feature: It helps the wall resist toppling and allows you to build thin walls higher than you could otherwise. The wall shown is only 4 inches thick.

To build a serpentine wall, cut plywood patterns in the shape of your planned curves. Hold a pattern up to the wall, and set the bricks slightly out of alignment to match the plywood curves. Check your local code for requirements for footings and reinforcement.

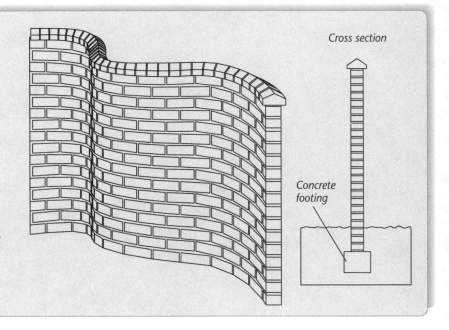

Cross section

Concrete footing

Each bond pattern requires a particular corner treatment. If you choose a pattern other than common bond, you'll need to adapt the instructions given on pages 28 to 30.

For English and Flemish bond, you will have to cut closure bricks: half bricks cut lengthwise, and one-quarter bricks cut widthwise.

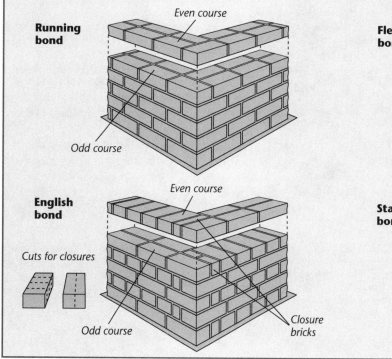

Running bond

Even course

Odd course

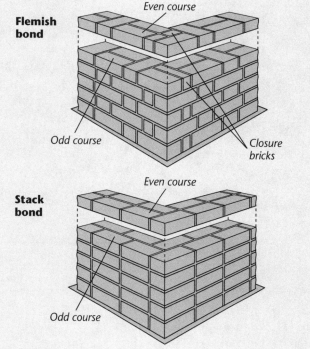

Flemish bond

Even course

Odd course

Closure bricks

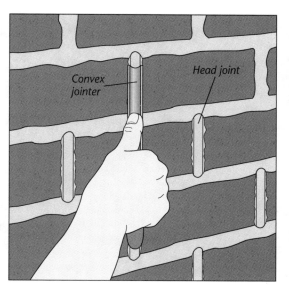

English bond

Even course

Cuts for closures

Odd course

Closure bricks

Stack bond

Even course

Odd course

Finishing mortar joints

TOOLKIT
- Striking tool
- Pointing trowel
- Stiff whisk brush

Convex jointer

Head joint

Bed joint

1 Striking the joints

If your job is small, tooling, or "striking," mortar joints can be left until the end. For larger jobs, though, you'll need to do this periodically as you work. Mortar joints should be struck when they are neither so soft that they smear the wall nor so hard that the metal tool leaves black marks; thumbprint hard is about right. See page 32 for the kinds of joints that can be struck with various tools. First, press or draw a striking tool vertically along each head joint as shown above left. Now run the striking tool horizontally along the bed joints *(above, right)*.

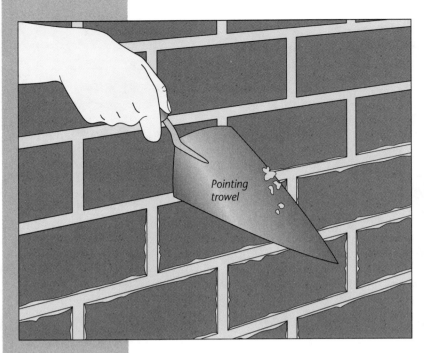

Pointing
trowel

2 Cutting off the tags and brushing the wall

Slide your trowel along the wall to remove the mortar that has been forced out of the joints, called tags. When you've finished, restrike the bed joints. Once the mortar is well set, brush the wall with a stiff broom or brush; this will eliminate the need for much later cleaning.

3 Cleaning up

Careful work is repaid at cleanup time. Try to keep mortar and dirt away from unit faces as you work. If brushing proves insufficient, wash with a solution of trisodium phosphate and laundry detergent. (Try $^1/_2$ cup of each for 1 gallon of water.) Rinse well. If this doesn't work, more drastic means—which are explained on page 88—may be necessary.

WHICH JOINT TOOLING?

Striking, or tooling, joints compacts and shapes the mortar, contributing to the strength and watertightness of the finished project. Some types of joints are more compacted or more watertight than others. Joint-striking tools (*page 19*) vary depending on the type of joint desired. They may be as simple as a piece of wood or copper tube. Popular mortar joints are illustrated here.

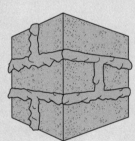

Extruded joint
Mortar is allowed to squeeze out (extrude) from the joint as the brick is laid. Has a rustic appearance but is not watertight; not suitable in rainy climates or where there is much freezing weather.

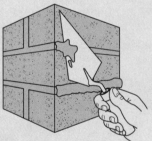

Flush joint
Made in the course of ordinary bricklaying; excess mortar is simply cut away with the trowel. Not a strong joint, since the mortar is not compacted; may not be watertight.

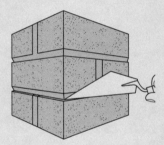

Struck joint
Joint is struck with the trowel, yielding some compacting. Provides for dramatic shadow lines but tends to collect water.

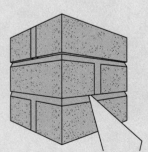

Weathered joint
Struck from below with the trowel. Most watertight joint of all and is somewhat compacted.

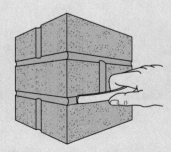

Concave joint
Made with a special jointer, as shown, or with a similar convex object. Readily sheds water and is well compacted.

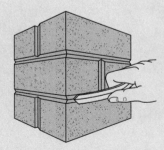

V-joint
Use a special tool as shown, or a metal bar, or a piece of wood. Similar to concave joint in strength and water resistance.

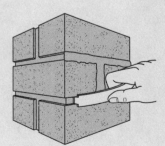

Raked joint
Use a joint raker for best results. Casts dramatic shadows. Water resistance is poor and joint is weaker than concave or V-joints.

BUILDING A CONCRETE BLOCK WALL

For fast, inexpensive masonry wall construction, it's hard to beat concrete blocks. These rugged units make strong decorative and structural walls, and working with them is usually well within the capacity of the do-it-yourselfer.

Designing block walls: Because concrete blocks are cast to such accurate sizes, you can plan with confidence. Cutting a block is hard to do without a power masonry saw, so it's best to pick the type of block first, then base the overall dimensions of the wall and its footing on the size of the block.

Check with your building department if the wall is to be more than 3 feet high. Codes may restrict your design above this height, and the instructions on pages 35 to 37 do not cover higher walls. For some suggestions on adding extra reinforcing to low walls see page 37.

To vary the look of your wall, consider using decorative blocks; see page 7 for some examples. Also, consider varying the bond pattern as explained on page 34.

Block size and weight: Remember that block dimensions are nominal; each measurement includes a standard 3/8-inch mortar joint. In addition to the 16-inch-long, 8-inch-wide standard size, blocks come in 4-, 6-, 10- and 12-inch widths. You might consider smaller widths if your wall is to be very low or larger ones if you want a massive effect.

Two weights of block are available. Standard blocks are molded with regular heavy aggregate and weigh about 45 pounds each. "Cinder" blocks, or lightweight blocks, are made with special lightweight aggregates and weigh considerably less. Either type is suitable for most residential projects, so you can make your selection on the basis of cost or your aching back.

Whatever the size and weight of the standard block, a whole series of fractional units is likely to be available to go with it. The standard block will probably be found in at least stretcher and corner forms *(right)*. It's easy to see that with a little planning and care in assembly, you'll never have to cut a block.

Mortarless blocks: A variety of concrete blocks are designed to be laid into the wall without mortar joints, saving a great deal

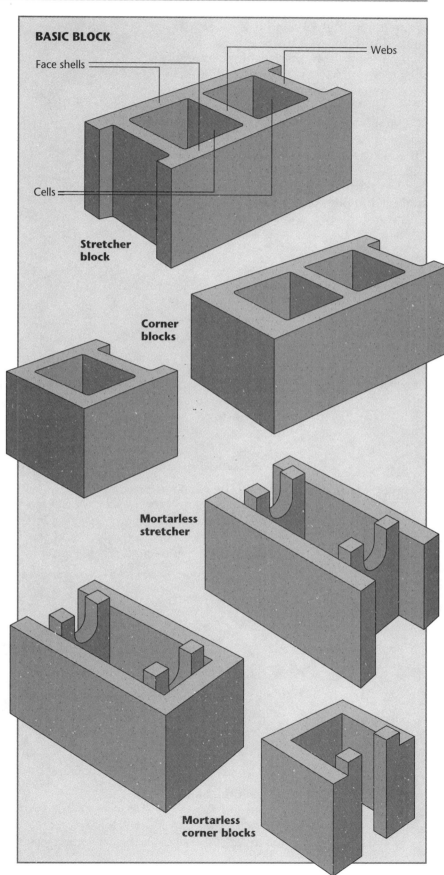

BASIC BLOCK

Face shells

Webs

Cells

Stretcher block

Corner blocks

Mortarless stretcher

Mortarless corner blocks

of effort. Once a mortarless block wall is reinforced and grouted it becomes as strong as one built with mortared blocks. The major drawback to mortarless blocks is the much higher cost of the specially shaped interlocking units.

In one popular mortarless-block system, the block units are available as 6- or 8-inch-wide stretchers, corners, and half corners *(page 33)*. Mortarless blocks are widely accepted by building codes and available in do-it-yourself outlets with leaflets describing how to lay them. Mortarless blocks are laid on cast-in-place footings. Laying them to a level stringline ensures a wall that is straight and plumb.

ASK A PRO

HOW DO I FIGURE OUT HOW MANY BLOCKS TO BUY?

It's a good idea to make an accurate drawing of your proposed project, showing the actual number of blocks per course and the number of courses. Then it will be easy to see how many blocks you'll need.

For example, a wall 8 feet long would require six standard blocks per course; two corner blocks and four stretchers. For running bond—the best bond to use for concrete blocks—every other course would begin and end with a half block and contain five standard stretchers.

Since each course is 8 inches high, it's easy to figure the number of courses needed to attain a given height, and thus the total number of each type of block you'll need. It's a good idea to order a few extra for waste.

Choosing a bond pattern

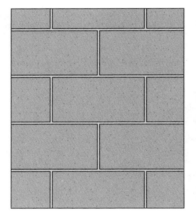
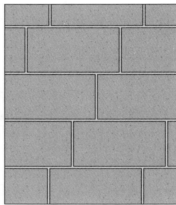
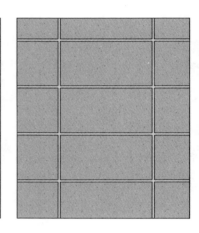

Varying the bond pattern

Basic bond patterns for concrete block include running bond *(above, left)*, offset running bond *(above, middle)*, and stack bond *(above, right)*. Stack bond requires extreme care in vertical joint alignment, as unevenness is easy to see. Running bond is most common, although stack bond, if well reinforced, is also used frequently. Both patterns allow cores to line up, making steel reinforcing and grouting easy.

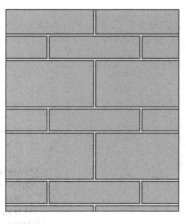
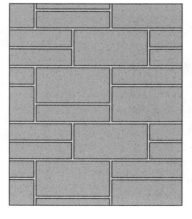
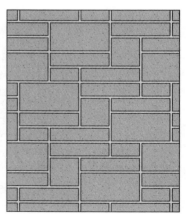

Varying the block size

Combining different sizes of block contributes to pattern interest: full-and half-height blocks *(above, left)*; the same blocks in a pattern reminiscent of ashlar stonework *(middle)*; and four sizes of split-face blocks in another ashlar pattern *(right)*. See page 41 for ashlar bonding patterns.

Erecting a block wall

TOOLKIT
- Mason's line
- Chalk line
- Tape measure
- Mortar board
- Mason's trowel
- Level
- Sled jointer

1 Building a footing and laying a dry course

Before digging the footing trench, lay out a dry course of blocks. Space them 3/8" apart, and plan the footing so that no block cutting will be necessary. Now install the footing; complete instructions appear on page 67. After the footing has cured for at least 2 days, you can start assembling the wall. Mark the foundation as you would for brickwork *(page 24)*.

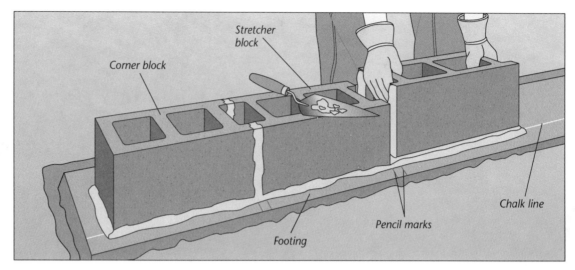

Corner block
Stretcher block
Footing
Pencil marks
Chalk line

2 Starting the lead

Use the same mortar that you would use for brick *(page 20)*. Keep the mortar a little on the stiff side; otherwise the heavy blocks may squeeze it out of the joints. Do not wet the blocks prior to laying them, as you would bricks. The stiffer mortar and the lower rate of absorption of the blocks will keep them from absorbing too much water from the mortar. Also, wetting makes the blocks expand, and later, when they dry, cracks will form in the wall.

Lay a 2" thick full mortar bed long enough for three or four blocks. Lay the corner block carefully and press it down to an accurate 3/8" joint with the foundation. Butter the ends of the next blocks; place them, allowing a 3/8" mortar joint. The face shells and webs are thicker on one side of the block than the other. Always lay blocks with the thick side up; it makes them easier to hold and gives more surface for the mortar bed. Check the lead for alignment, level, and plumb.

Half block
Chalk line
Level

3 Completing the lead

Continue as for bricklaying *(page 26)*, beginning even-numbered courses with half blocks. For maximum strength, you can mortar both the face shells and webs, making full bed joints; otherwise, mortar just the face shells. When one lead is finished, go to the other end of the wall and build the second lead.

4 ▶ Filling in between leads

Lay blocks between the leads, keeping a careful check on the ³/₈" joint spacing. Be sure to check alignment, level, and plumb frequently. To fit the closure block, spread mortar on all edges of the opening and the ends of the block, then carefully set it in place.

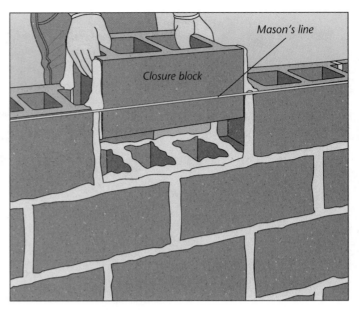

Mason's line

Closure block

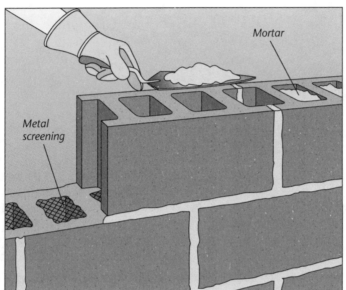

Mortar

Metal screening

5 ▶ Capping the wall

You can make a simple cap by filling the cores of the top course with mortar. First cover the cores of the next-to-last course with ¹/₄" metal screening or building paper before laying the top course. Be sure the building paper doesn't interfere with the bond between the face shells. Then add the mortar *(left)*.

6 ▶ Installing a decorative cap

Solid cap blocks in various thicknesses are available; these help give the wall a more finished look. Simply mortar them in place on full bed joints.

Cap block

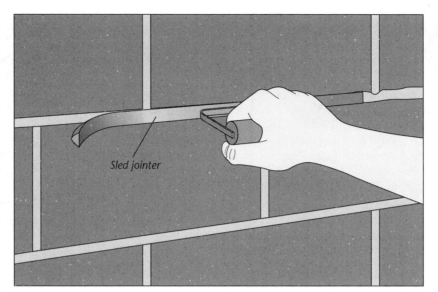

Sled jointer

7 **Finishing the joints**

For the greatest strength, use a compacted concave or V-shaped joint. A long sled jointer like the one shown is best, but a smaller jointer, or even a dowel, will do. Tool the vertical, then the horizontal joints, working from bottom to top. Finish by knocking off tags with your trowel *(page 32)*.

BUILDING EXTRA STRENGTH INTO A BLOCK WALL

Concrete block walls higher than 3 feet require a great deal of steel reinforcing that is likely to be difficult for a beginner. However, you may want to add some reinforcement to even the low walls we have shown here, especially if the wall will be exposed to high winds or possibly the impact of a car—or even a bicycle. The simplest approach is to include a bond-beam cast into the wall at the top, as shown. Special bond-beam blocks are available with cutaway webs to allow the placement of reinforcing rods and grout. Or, you can make your own bond-beam blocks by knocking the webs out of standard units—but be sure to place 1/4-inch metal screen or building paper under them to retain the grout. Once the grout sets up around the steel, the top of the wall becomes a monolithic beam that greatly strengthens the wall.

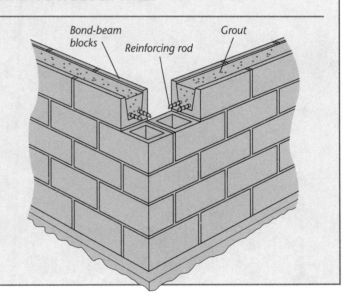

Bond-beam blocks

Reinforcing rod

Grout

ASK A PRO

WHAT IF I HAVE TO CUT A CONCRETE BLOCK?

Cut a block first by scoring both sides with a brickset (page 26). You can also use a rented power masonry saw, or a circular saw with a masonry cutoff blade. When cutting masonry with a circular saw, always wear goggles; a face shield is also a good idea in case the blade snaps. Make a series of cuts, going deeper each time. Place the saw's base plate on the block; make sure that the power cord or extension is clear of the path. Turn the motor on and wait until it has reached speed. Carefully begin cutting. Follow the cutting line slowly without forcing the blade; stop if the saw vibrates or makes unusual noises. Once through the cut, turn the saw off, and wait for the blade to stop before preparing to cut at the next depth.

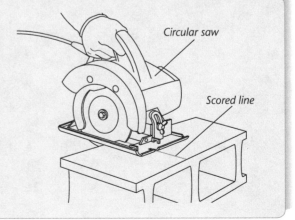

Circular saw

Scored line

BUILDING AN ADOBE WALL

Nothing adds regional flavor to a garden like adobe. This simple mud brick was probably the first building material to be manufactured by human beings, and it is still used today. Cement and asphalt stabilizers now make the blocks waterproof and have contributed to the gradual acceptance of adobe outside its native Southwest. When used in a garden setting, the rugged earthen blocks harmonize well with most kinds of plantings. Here, we will show how to make a simple garden wall, but don't overlook indoor applications—sturdy hearths and fireplaces, for example, have been made of adobe for hundreds of years.

Sizes of blocks: Adobe blocks come in several sizes, as shown opposite. Blocks are generally 4 inches thick by 16 inches long, the width varying from 4 to 12 inches. The most common block is 4 x 8 x 16 inches, about the same as four or five clay bricks. (Block thicknesses include the mortar joint.) Because the blocks are large, adobe wall construction proceeds quickly, and your efforts yield rapid results.

Laying adobe blocks: Laying up an adobe wall is similar to building with concrete blocks or bricks. Running bond is the pattern almost always used. Because of their weight, you'll need a sturdy footing for adobe blocks, as shown below. Adobe walls do not need to be reinforced.

Cutting the blocks to fit is easy. Use the procedure for cutting bricks shown on page 26. Or try an old hatchet or a saw—sometimes these work just as well.

Mortar: Adobe mortar is used in traditional adobe construction, but best practice today calls for portland cement mortar, especially if you're using stabilized

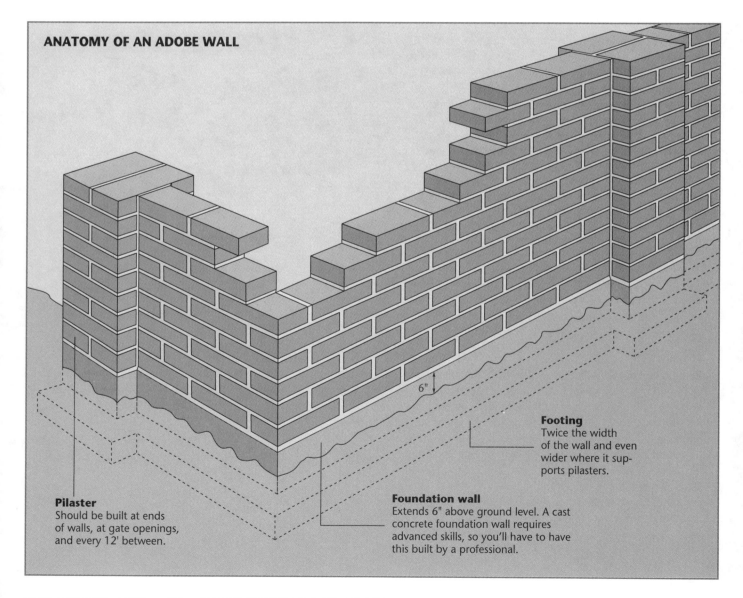

ANATOMY OF AN ADOBE WALL

6"

Footing
Twice the width of the wall and even wider where it supports pilasters.

Pilaster
Should be built at ends of walls, at gate openings, and every 12' between.

Foundation wall
Extends 6" above ground level. A cast concrete foundation wall requires advanced skills, so you'll have to have this built by a professional.

adobe blocks. Use a leaner mixture (one with less cement) than for bricklaying. The formula for adobe mortar is one part cement to two parts soil to three parts sand. Add 1½ gallons asphalt emulsion per sack of cement to waterproof the joints. The added soil gives the mortar an adobe color and "leans" the mix.

Ideally, the soil added to the mortar should be the same as that used for the blocks. This is no problem if you live near the manufacturer. Don't use clay soil—the type often called "adobe." Many clays are detrimental to mortar and to the blocks. The proper soil and the asphalt emulsion are available from your supplier. You can color the mortar by adding oxides as you mix it. See your dealer for available colors and proportions.

How to order adobe blocks: If your local building materials yard doesn't carry a sufficient supply of adobe, they can order for you from an adobe manufacturer. Or you can order directly from an adobe manufacturer and have the blocks sent to you direct; be sure to inquire about freight charges. You might also make your own arrangements with a hauling contractor.

Using the 4 x 7½ x 16-inch block to build a nominal 8-inch-thick wall, order as follows for each 100 square feet of wall:

Adobe blocks	200
Sand (cubic feet)	9
Portland cement (sacks)	3½
Asphalt stabilizer (gallons)	5½

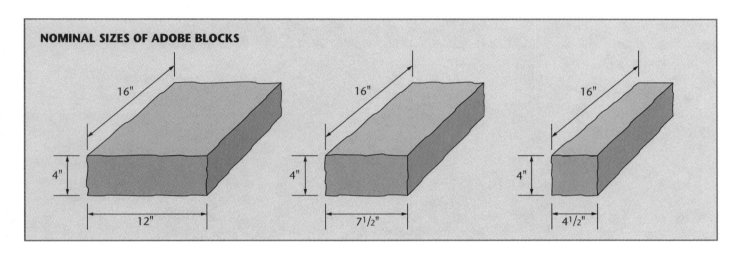

NOMINAL SIZES OF ADOBE BLOCKS

16" 4" 12"

16" 4" 7½"

16" 4" 4½"

Constructing an adobe wall

TOOLKIT
• Hawk
• Mason's trowel
• Mason's line
• Level
• Steel trowel
• Tape measure
• Chalk line

Mason's line

Mason's trowel

1 **Laying the block**
Refer to pages 24-27 for basic instructions on bricklaying. The method is essentially the same with adobe; only the scale is different. As shown above, you use more mortar, and the blocks are much larger and heavier. Use a mason's line and work from leads, as you would for a brick or concrete block wall, maintaining a ½" mortar joint.

2 Filling in between leads

Once the leads are completed, fill in each course between the leads as you would for brick *(page 26)*. Make sure to check frequently for alignment, level, and plumb with a mason's level.

3 Building a corner

Since adobe is laid in a running bond pattern, corners are easy to deal with and no cutting of adobe blocks is required. Interlock the blocks at the corner as shown.

4 Finishing the surface

Mortar joints can be tooled as for brick *(page 31)*, or struck off flush with the blocks using a steel trowel for a characteristic Southwestern look, as shown here.

Traditionally, adobe was plastered and covered with a coat of whitewash for waterproofing. Nowadays, however, stabilized adobe requires no finish at all and once you plaster or paint your wall, its rustic appearance is lost.

If you do decide to paint, use exterior latex (water-base) paints. Don't use oil-base paints, since they may dissolve some of the asphalt stabilizer.

BUILDING A STONE WALL

More than any other masonry material, stone lends an aura of permanence to a structure. Stonework ranges in appearance from the casual look of countryside rubble walls to the formality of exactly fitted ashlar masonry. In the next six pages you'll find complete instructions for building 3-foot-high stone walls; see pages 49 to 61 for paving with stone.

To begin, turn to page 10 to choose which kind of stone you will use. Then decide on the type of stonework—rubble or ashlar—and whether the wall will be laid dry or mortared. If you choose a mortared wall, you will first have to construct a concrete footing *(page 67)*; dry-laid walls may be built directly on the ground.

Because stone walls cannot be reinforced easily, building codes in areas subject to earthquakes generally frown on stone masonry. In these locations stone walls may be restricted to facing a reinforced concrete wall. However, if you keep your stone walls under 3 feet high, earthquake damage should be held to a minimum.

Types of stonework: There are two broad classes of stonework—rubble and ashlar. Between these extremes you'll find all sorts of "roughly squared" stonework, where some trimming of the stones has been done. Cobblestones are an example.

Stones used for **rubble masonry** are often rounded from glacial or water action and include river rock and fieldstone. The rocks are often of igneous origin—hardheaded granite and basalt. Because they're tough to cut, it's usually easier to search for the right-sized rock.

Rubble stonework is built up without courses, designed to achieve a pleasing arrangement of different sizes, as shown at right. Because of the irregular spaces between the stones, much more mortar is required than for ashlar construction. Rubble stone can also be laid dry, with the stones holding each other in place by weight and friction. This is usually the cheapest method—sometimes it's even free. The famous New England dry stone walls were built by farmers in the course of clearing their fields.

Fully trimmed **ashlar stone** can be nearly as easy to lay as brick. The flat surfaces and

BONDING PATTERNS

Untrimmed rubble stone
Can be laid "dry" *(above, left)*, or with mortar *(above, right)*. Crevice plantings give the dry wall a natural look. Vertical (head) joints are always staggered, for maximum strength.

Roughly squared stones
Some trimming is done at the quarry. Laid without regular courses *(above, left)*, the effect is similar to a mortared rubble wall. Laying the stones in regular horizontal courses *(above, right)*, gives a look resembling ashlar stonework.

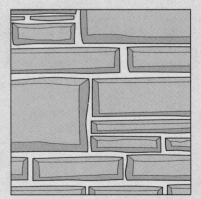

Ashlar stone
Can be laid either without regular coursing *(above, left)* or with coursing *(above, right)*. Head joints are always staggered. Avoiding regular courses gives a more rustic effect; including them makes the wall more formal looking.

limited range of sizes make coursing possible and require less mortar than for rubble work. You can get a less formal effect by avoiding regular courses, as shown on page 41, and still take advantage of the labor-saving qualities of the cut stones.

The stone used is usually sedimentary in origin—sandstone is probably the most common. The stratification of the stone makes it easy to split and trim. It's softer and less durable than igneous rock, but this is of little concern in nonstructural applications. When an igneous stone such as granite is cut and trimmed for ashlar masonry, costs are likely to be quite high.

Bonding in stone walls: As you work, be sure that vertical joints are staggered; there should always be an overlap with the stones above and below.

Freestanding walls are usually laid up in two rough wythes with rubble fill. Bond stones, equivalent to headers in brickwork *(page 25)*, run across the wall, tying it together. You should use as many bond stones as possible—at least one for every 10 square feet of wall surface.

Most stone walls should slope inward (toward the center) on both surfaces. This tilting of the faces is called batter and helps secure the wall, since the faces lean on each other. A good rule of thumb for a mortared wall is 1 to 2 inches of batter for every 2 feet of rise; less if the stones are very regular. Unmortared walls should have 3 to 4 inches of batter for every 2 feet of rise. Ashlar stonework does not require batter.

Buying stone: Buy your stone from a reputable dealer. Avoid stone that was blasted out of the ground as it contains tiny fissures that will encourage deterioration of the wall. If you figure the cubic volume of your wall, your dealer can calculate the quantity of stone you'll need. Some dealers sell by the cubic yard, simplifying your order; others sell by the ton. To find the volume of your wall, multiply its height by its width by its length. Stone usually weighs in the region of 125 pounds per cubic foot.

Rubble stone will have a greater volume per ton than trimmed stone because of the voids between the rocks. When it is loaded in a truck, rubble stone might run as much as three parts rock to one part void—25 percent air. Once you begin fitting the stones into a wall, you'll find their volume considerably reduced. Try to inspect before you buy. Stones should harmonize in color and texture and should show a good range of sizes. For best effect, the face area of the largest stones should be about six times the face area of the smallest.

Trimmed stones are ordered by their width and thickness, and you should specify the upper and lower limits of length desired.

MAKING A BATTER GAUGE

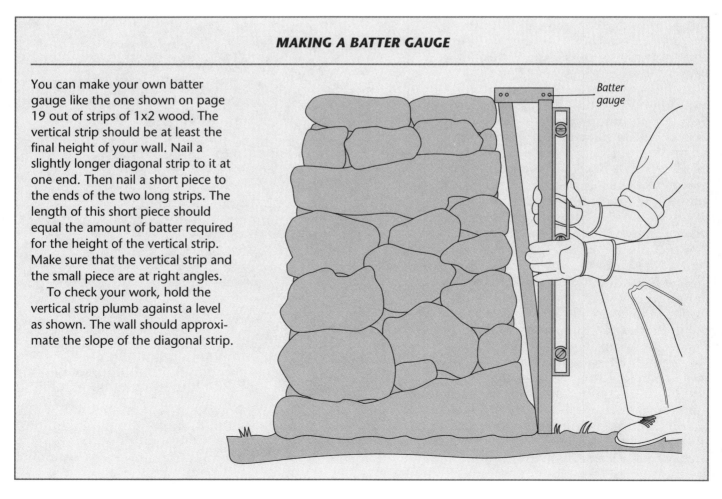

You can make your own batter gauge like the one shown on page 19 out of strips of 1x2 wood. The vertical strip should be at least the final height of your wall. Nail a slightly longer diagonal strip to it at one end. Then nail a short piece to the ends of the two long strips. The length of this short piece should equal the amount of batter required for the height of the vertical strip. Make sure that the vertical strip and the small piece are at right angles.

To check your work, hold the vertical strip plumb against a level as shown. The wall should approximate the slope of the diagonal strip.

Batter gauge

Erecting a dry stone wall

TOOLKIT
- Shovel
- Batter gauge
- Level
- Stone chisel or brickset
- Hand-drilling hammer

1 Planning the wall

Plan on a battered wall no higher than it is thick at its base. Very round stones will require so much batter that the resulting dry wall may be no higher than a third of its thickness. Even in severe frost areas, dry walls are built in very shallow trenches without footings. Since the wall is flexible, frost heaves tend to dislodge only a few stones, which can be easily replaced.

Select your largest stones for the foundation course to spare your back and strengthen the wall.

2 Laying the first course

Lay the foundation stones in a shallow trench; this will help stabilize the wall. Begin with a bond stone—a stone the width of the wall—and then start the two face courses. Try to lay stones flat, as they occur naturally. Fill the center with rubble.

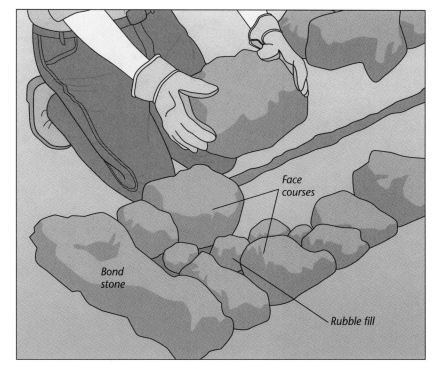

Face courses

Bond stone

Rubble fill

Batter gauge

3 Laying the second course

Lay stones on top of the first course, being sure that vertical joints do not line up. Stones of each face should tilt inward toward each other. Use your batter gauge and level on sides and ends to maintain proper slope. Again, fill the center with rubble.

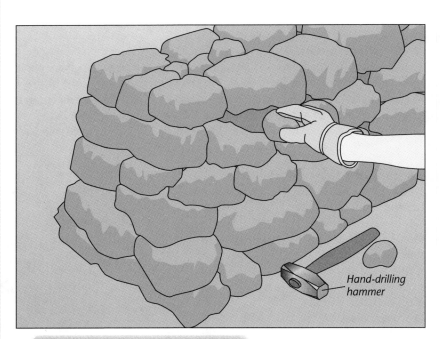

4 Adding additional courses

Continue in the same manner, maintaining an inward tilt so that gravity will hold the wall together. Place bond stones every 5-10 square feet. Use small stones to fill large gaps; if you tap them in with a hammer, the wall will be stronger. But don't overdo it—driving them in too far will actually weaken the structure.

Hand-drilling hammer

 ASK A PRO

HOW DO I CUT A STONE?

First of all, always wear safety goggles. To fit an awkwardly shaped stone, a certain amount of trimming can be done simply by hammering at the stone with a bricklayer's hammer. If you need to cut a stone, a stone chisel or brickset will work. Score a line completely around the stone, tapping the chisel with a hand-drilling hammer. Then drive the chisel against the line to break the stone apart; try to work with the natural fissures in the stone.

Large, flat stone

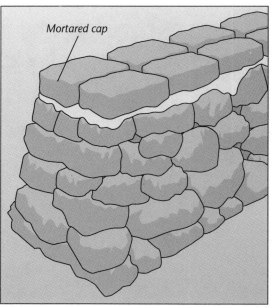

Mortared cap

5 Laying the top course

Save your flattest, broadest stones for the top. If you live in an area with severe freezing, consider mortaring the cap as shown above; this will drain water away from the wall and help prevent frost damage.

Putting up a mortared stone wall

1 Planning the wall

Any kind of stone can be mortared into a stable wall. The quantity of mortar increases sharply with progressively rounder stones. A wall 2' thick can safely be built without batter to a height of about 5'. Many municipalities do require an engineered plan and a building permit for walls over 3', so be sure to check. (The following instructions cover walls 3' high or less.) You'll need a concrete footing *(page 67)* extending below the frost line; in frost-free areas, a 12" deep footing is sufficient for a 3' wall. Bring concrete to within an inch or so of ground level. The footing should be about half again as wide as the wall.

2 Mixing mortar

The mortar formula for stonework contains more cement than that used for brick or block *(page 20)*: one part cement to three or four parts sand. You can add one half part fireclay (available from your building supplier) for workability, but don't add lime (or mortar cement, which contains lime) because it might stain the stones. Keep the mortar somewhat stiffer than for brick or block.

ASK A PRO

HOW MUCH MORTAR DO I NEED?

Because of its large joints and voids, a rubble stone wall may be as much as one-third mortar. To plan for this, lay up a small section of the wall, note the amount of mortar used, and use this as a guide for the rest. It's not a bad idea to use this method even if you're working with well-trimmed stone. Every stone wall is a special case; laying a sample section will be your best guide to the amount of mortar you'll need.

3 Starting the first course

Your stones should be clean and dry (dirt and moisture interfere with the bond). First lay a 1" thick mortar bed for the first bond stone and set it in place. Continue as for a dry wall *(page 43, step 2)*, mortaring the edges of the stones before laying them, and then filling in the center with rubble and mortar. Pack the head joints (vertical joints) with mortar after setting the stones.

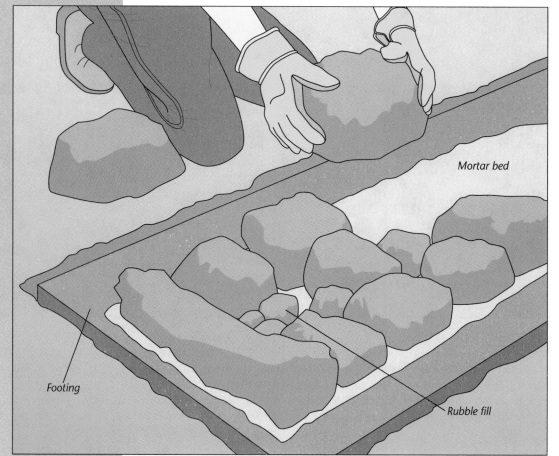

Mortar bed

Footing

Rubble fill

 4 Laying additional courses

For each subsequent course, build up a mortar bed and set the stones in place just as you did to begin. Work slowly, dry-fitting stones before throwing down the mortar. You can save mortar by filling large joints with small stones and chips. Check the wall's alignment and plumb or batter *(page 42)* as you go.

ASK A PRO

HOW DO I SUPPORT VERY HEAVY STONES?

Very large stones may squeeze out all the mortar in their bed joints. To preserve joint spacing, support them on wooden wedges. After the mortar is stiff, you can pull out the wedges and pack the holes with mortar. Stone chips may also be used as wedges inside the wall.

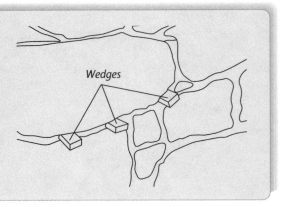

Wedges

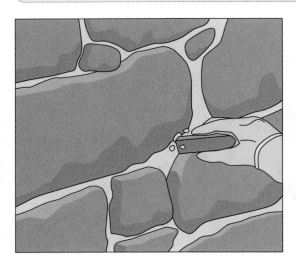

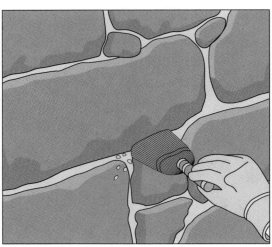

5 Raking the joints

After you've laid a section, use a piece of wood to rake out the joints to a depth of 1/2" to 3/4" *(above)*. Deeply raked mortar joints enhance the play of light and shadow on the face of the wall. Ashlar stone walls can be struck as for brick *(page 31)*.

6 Cleaning up

Spilled mortar should be wiped from the face of the stone with a wet sponge as you work. After the mortar joints are tooled, use a broom or brush to remove crumbs of mortar. Once the mortar has dried, wash the wall with clear water. If this doesn't work, try soapy water and a clear rinse. Don't use a steel brush—it could mar the stone.

RETAINING WALLS

Most municipalities require a permit for any retaining wall over 2 feet, because the quality of construction and design is critical. Many also specify that walls over 4 feet high must be designed and supervised by a licensed engineer. Thus you must consult your building department any time you are planning a project on a more ambitious scale than a low garden terrace, planting bed, or tree well.

The discussion that follows is an introduction to retaining walls—walls that hold up a higher level of earth. On page 48 is an example of a concrete-block retaining wall built to typical specifications; it may or may not meet your local specifications.

PREPARING THE SLOPE
Even the gentlest of slopes requires some alteration before a wall can be built, and appropriate planting helps control erosion.

Cutting and filling: The drawing below shows three typical methods of site preparation. In the first, the slope is cut away and the earth moved downhill to create a plateau. In the second, a raised bed is created by cutting away below the wall site and filling on the uphill side. The third method divides the total wall height into two smaller walls, creating terraces—usually the best idea wherever possible.

Planting: Hardy, firm-rooted plants that cover well but won't spread too fast to control will also help to retain the soil. It's best to plant right away after completing the retaining wall, while the soil is still soft and easily worked.

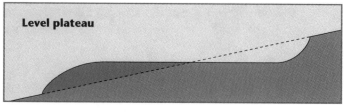

Level plateau

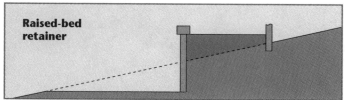

Raised-bed retainer

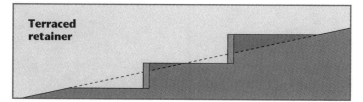

Terraced retainer

WATER CONTROL
Drainage is an essential part of retaining-wall design. Once rains have saturated the soil, water flows downhill, both above and below the ground. Your retaining wall acts like a dam, restricting this flow of water. You must make some provision for drainage or risk undermining or even bursting the wall.

If you are dealing with expansive clay soil, you have an additional problem. The saturated soil expands and acts like a hydraulic jack, pressing against the wall. In this case, professional engineering is called for.

Drainage: The drawing on the next page shows a typical drainage scheme, with drain pipes passing through the wall. The tarpaper covering the gravel backfill prevents the soil from sifting down from above into the gravel and clogging it.

RETAINING-WALL DESIGNS
There are two basic types of retaining-wall designs: mass and cantilever. A mass wall is held in place by the simple pressure of its mass; the force of gravity does the work. A cantilever wall relies on the strength of steel reinforcing; this design has an extremely wide foundation to help it resist toppling and "sledding"—the tendency to slide outward because of the pressure that is exerted by the earth.

Retaining walls can be built from a variety of materials, although engineering must take precedence over appearance in most cases. Here are the pros and cons of the masonry materials most often used in retaining walls:

Cast concrete: Strongest of all, concrete walls stand where other types of wall fail. The cost of formwork for large walls can become prohibitive for residential projects, however.

Concrete block: Solid-grouted, reinforced concrete-block cantilever walls, as shown on the next page, are nearly as strong as the cast concrete kind; the units act as permanent forms for the grout. This is usually the most economical form of construction, small or large. Appearance can be enhanced by veneering or by varying the bond pattern *(page 34)*.

In the example shown, the foundation is cast first, with steel reinforcing incorporated. Then the wall is erected, using bond-beam blocks and horizontal reinforcing in every other course. Every other block in the lowest bond-beam course is notched to receive plastic pipe *(inset)*. The pipes form weep holes for drainage. Grouting is done in stages as each bond-beam course is completed. A mortar cap completes the project.

A $3/4$-inch coat of mortar, called a parge coat, trowelled onto the back of the wall, will help to control dampness on the face. Heavy tarpaper or a special rubber membrane will do the same thing.

Brick: Brick retaining walls are attractive but are weaker than the concrete varieties. They are usually laid up in two tiers, or wythes, with steel reinforcement between them *(page 24)*. Grout is used to fill the cavity, locking in the steel and strengthening the wall. Often, the inner wythe is built of inexpensive concrete blocks, which make for greater speed of construction as well as cost savings.

Stone: Thick, mortared stone retaining walls are stronger than the brick type, mostly because of the extra thickness. Dry-laid stone walls have a rough-hewn beauty and make attractive retainers. Because these dry-laid walls are not mortared, they should be tilted back into the slope—battered—to increase their holding power. The joints can be planted to enhance the wall's appearance.

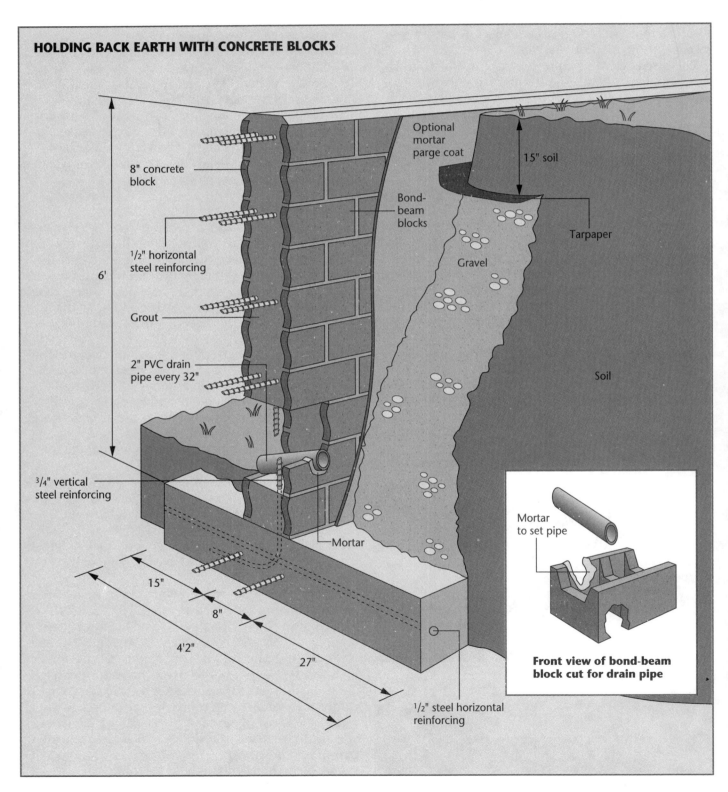

HOLDING BACK EARTH WITH CONCRETE BLOCKS

- 8" concrete block
- 1/2" horizontal steel reinforcing
- 6'
- Grout
- 2" PVC drain pipe every 32"
- 3/4" vertical steel reinforcing
- 15"
- 8"
- 4'2"
- 27"
- Mortar
- 1/2" steel horizontal reinforcing
- Optional mortar parge coat
- Bond-beam blocks
- 15" soil
- Tarpaper
- Gravel
- Soil

Mortar to set pipe

Front view of bond-beam block cut for drain pipe

PAVING: BRICK, PAVERS, STONE, AND TILE

Every home needs some paving, whether it is an elegant patio suitable for lavish entertaining or just a modest walkway alongside the house. Whatever your needs, some form of masonry—either cast concrete, as shown beginning on page 62, or unit-type—is likely to be the answer.

Unit masonry—brick, pavers, stone, and tile—offers the easiest approach, and the results can be durable and truly handsome. Preparations are generally simple, and building need not be completed all at once; it can proceed on a weekend-by-weekend basis.

Unit paving will probably be more expensive than cast concrete for very large areas, but for small- to medium-size jobs, working with units can really pay off. The simplicity of laying brick in sand, for example, may more than offset its cost when you consider that you are not contending with a concrete truck and can work at your own convenience and pace.

Today's paving units offer you a wide range of effects. As you can see on the next page, your choice of material has quite a dramatic impact on the "feel" of your completed project. After you've established the location and scope of your project, choose materials carefully; once they're down, they're likely to be down for some time. Tools you're likely to need are shown on page 19; you'll also need a tamper, shown on page 63. For information on working safely with materials, see page 18.

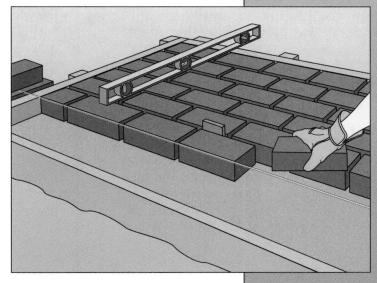

Brick paving will beautify any walkway, and laying bricks in wet mortar is not as difficult as you might think. (See page 58 for how-to instructions.)

49

BEFORE YOU BEGIN

Here are some factors to keep in mind when choosing paving materials. Consult the first chapter for information on each material.

•**Surface texture:** Smooth, shiny surfaces can be slippery when wet, and rougher ones too absorbent for use near a barbecue. Smooth surfaces are best for dancing; games require surfaces with more traction. You'll need a hard-wearing surface if furniture will be dragged across it, but a softer one will do for foot traffic.

•**Appearance:** Consider your taste in color, texture, pattern, and reflective quality. Dull surfaces mean less glare on the sunny side of the house; shiny surfaces can catch the light on the shady side.

•**Maintenance:** Most surfaces can be simply hosed down or swept, but some may show dirt more than others and need attention more often. Large mortar joints may trap debris, yet shed water well. Sanded joints are easy to maintain but may allow weeds to grow through.

•**Durability:** Consider wear from both climate and use. On stable soil, brick in sand is a permanent paving, but in areas with extreme freezing, you may get tired of reworking the bricks every spring.

•**Cost:** Consider more than just the material itself. Labor will vary, and hidden costs may lurk in such things as drainage, unstable soil, or special construction methods.

•**Application:** Consider how to get your materials to the jobsite. If you have to carry everything by hand, you may not want to use really heavy blocks. Schedule your work for the best season, and try to anticipate the amount of help you'll need—also the amount of inconvenience you're willing to put up with as the work is proceeding. It's not a bad idea to double your time estimate.

SAME PROJECT, DIFFERENT MATERIALS

Brick laid in running bond
A simple, traditional surface that harmonizes with the low seating wall.

Brick laid in other patterns
Divides the single expanse and defines areas.

Mellow adobe
Its rounded, massive form looks good with crevice planting.

Tile paving
Gives a more formal effect and a smoother, more reflective surface.

Rugged stone
Resists stains and scratches. Gives a rough-hewn effect.

Interlocking pavers.
Very durable. Special edging pieces make cutting unnecessary.

CHOOSING A METHOD

Masonry units can be laid either in sand or by using either the dry- or wet-mortar method.

Laying masonry units in sand: This is a simple method that yields surprisingly sturdy results. Typically, once the surface is graded, a strong edge is built, either with mortared masonry, cast concrete, or lumber *(page 52)*. A sand bed is then poured in and leveled, and the units are placed tightly together, filling the area.

The secret of the strength of this paving lies in the last step. Sand is swept into the narrow joints between units, where each grain acts like a tiny wedge to lock the units together. An occasional resanding improves the wedging effect; traffic moves the units slightly, forcing the sand ever deeper into the joints and the whole pavement even tighter against its restraining edges. If the edges hold and the ground doesn't move, this paving is simple and permanent. You can expect some settling over time, so it's a good idea to build a little high to allow for it. Occasional weeds in the joints can be kept down with a contact weed killer, or you can lay plastic sheeting between the bricks and the underlying sand.

Sand-bedding the units provides a flexible surface that allows for easy repair should tree roots or freezing weather cause the underlying surface to buckle. Also, if a unit is damaged, it can be replaced easily if it has been laid in sand.

Mortared paving, dry or wet: Added stability is gained when you work with mortar. Brick laid in wet mortar over a concrete slab *(page 58)* provides the best protection against frost heaves and weed invasion. The dry-mortar method provides some of this permanence with a lot less effort.

WORKING WITH PAVING UNITS

Your choice of method for laying unit paving is partly dependent on the type of material you're using.

Bricks can be laid in sand or in wet or dry mortar. Although a hard winter may cause a brick-in-sand surface to buckle, repair is easy; pick up the offenders, re-level the sand bed, and re-lay the bricks. For cutting bricks, see page 26.

Pavers are laid in sand; alignment is nearly automatic. Non-interlocking, rectangular concrete pavers can be set in either sand or dry mortar. Pavers can be cut with a masonry saw, a circular saw with a cut-off blade, or a guillotine.

Adobe paving blocks are usually laid in sand with 1-inch sanded or dirt-filled joints. The large joints help make up for size variations, improve drainage, and allow for crevice planting. Cut adobe the same way as you do brick *(page 26)*.

Tiles can be laid in sand or dry mortared, but are best mortared over concrete slabs and wood decks. Tiles can be cut with a tile cutter or a tile nipper *(page 19)*.

Flagstone is one of the few materials that can be laid directly on stable soil as well as in sand or mortar. The large size and weight of the stones add to their stability. For instructions on cutting flagstone, turn to page 60.

PLENTY OF PATTERNS

A brick path or patio can be graceful as well as sturdy. As the illustrations show, this simple form lends itself to a broad range of paving patterns.

Running bond

Jack on jack

Basket weave

Herringbone

Diagonal herringbone/jack on jack

Basket weave/grid system

BUILDING EDGINGS

Edgings border and retain paving units, keeping them from moving, so they are the key to security—especially when pavement is laid in sand. Here we show you four basic methods of building edgings: wooden edgings, shown below; brick-in-soil edgings, on page 53; and invisible and concrete edgings, on page 54. Edgings can be built either before or after grading; here we assume that grading is completed first (below). Install the edgings before beginning to pave. Edgings are not required with flagstone or with the wet-mortar method.

Preparing the base

TOOLKIT
- Pointed shovel
- String
- Small sledgehammer to drive in stakes
- Chalk line
- Mason's level or line level
- Tamper

1 Planning drainage
Stable masonry paving requires a well-prepared base of firm, well-drained soil. Paving an area affects its drainage—water will run off even the most porous paving, such as brick-in-sand. Unless the area slopes naturally, you must grade it so that runoff will not collect where it will cause problems—against a house foundation, for example. You should provide a pitch of at least 1" in 10'.

Avoid sending the runoff toward any place that is already boggy during a rain. Refer such a problem to a landscape contractor or an architect.

2 Grading
When grading, you'll usually dig out the area to be paved. Plan to avoid filling and tamping; tamped earth is never as firm as undisturbed soil.

To grade the area, first stake it off in squares of 5' or 10'; use a taut string to align the stakes. Mark your preferred level for the finished paving surface on one stake. This should be at or above existing grade. Attach a chalk line at this point and stretch it along a row of stakes. Level the line and snap it to mark the stakes. Repeat for all the stakes.

Now adjust your marks to allow for a pitch of 1" in 10'. Plan to have the low side of the paving end at or above the natural ground level, not below it, by measuring down on the stakes at the low end or up on the stakes at the high end or both. Using the chalk line, mark the stakes again.

Excavate below your marks a distance equal to the paving thickness plus the thickness of the setting bed. If you must fill, use sand and tamp it. (See the illustration of a tamper on page 63). Grading can also be done after edging, using the edgings as guides.

Building a wooden edging

TOOLKIT
- String
- Mason's level or line level.
- Pointed shovel
- Hand-drilling hammer or small sledgehammer
- Hammer
- Saw

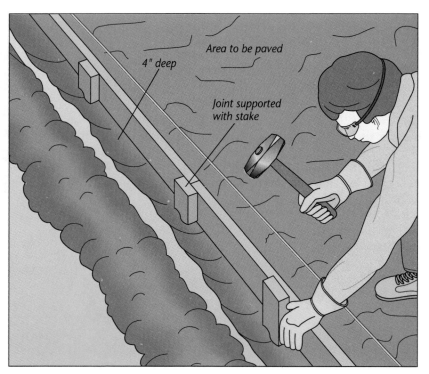

Area to be paved

4" deep

Joint supported with stake

1 Constructing the edging
After grading, drive 2 stakes and stretch a guideline to mark the edging height. Level the line with a mason's level or a line level. Then, drive in 18" to 24" pointed stakes and nail on the edging. For the edges that slope, drive successive stakes (left) a little lower than the string to achieve desired slope. Use 2x4 redwood, cedar heartwood, or pressure-treated lumber (treated to ground-contact rating) for both stakes and edging.

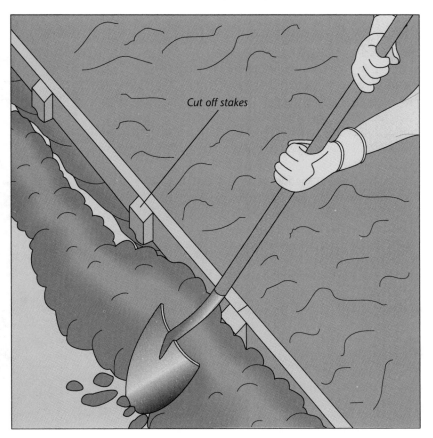

2 Filling in
Cut off the tops of the stakes at an angle, as shown, then fill in to the outer edge with soil (this will hide the stakes). The rest of the area will be dug to at least as deep as the inner part of the trench that has already been dug.

Cut off stakes

Building a brick-in-soil edging

TOOLKIT
• 4" spade
• Level

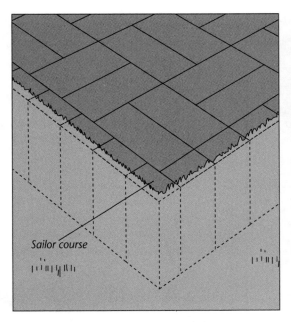

Sailor course

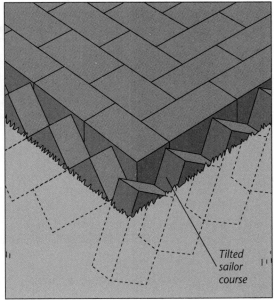

Tilted sailor course

Constructing two types of edgings

Brick-in-soil edgings are the easiest to construct, but the earth must be really firm and capable of holding the bricks securely. For the type of edging shown above left, cut a narrow trench deep enough to bury the full length of a brick (unless the area has already been graded deep enough). Install a row of "sailors"—bricks standing on end—leveling the tops as you go. Pack earth tightly against the outer perimeter of the bricks to secure them.

For the type of edging shown above right, install the sailor course tilted at 45°. This gives a notched effect at the edge and allows the pavement to rise above grade, at the same time keeping as much of the brick edging underground as possible.

Building an invisible edging

TOOLKIT
- 4" spade
- Strikeoff
- Hammer
- Small sledgehammer to drive in stakes
- Rubber mallet

1 ▶ Casting the concrete

"Invisible" edgings rely on a small concrete footing to hold them in place. This is a strong type of edging that is effective with brick-in-sand paving and adaptable to interlocking concrete pavers, regular paving blocks, and other units.

Place concrete *(page 67)* between temporary form boards made of 2x8 lumber, set one brick length apart, and nailed to 2x2 or 1x4 stakes. Use a strikeoff to level the concrete 1 brick-thickness below the top of the form (The concrete should be about 4" thick.) As you move the strikeoff along, place bricks in the plastic concrete. Set them with a few taps of a rubber mallet.

These edgings can be adapted to other types of units by adjusting the distance between the form boards and the depth of the top of the concrete below the surface.

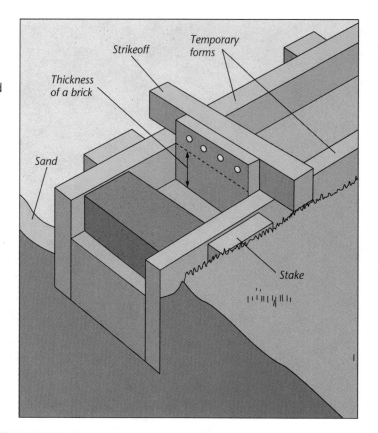

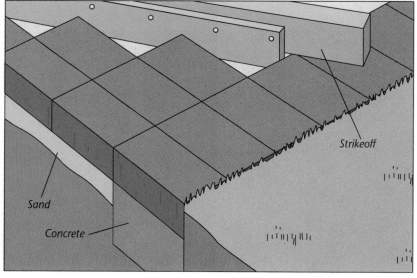

◀ 2 Leveling the sand

The next day, remove the form. After the concrete has cured, use the completed edging as a guide to strike off the sand, and then begin the brick-in-sand paving.

Building a concrete edging

TOOLKIT
- 4" spade
- Small sledgehammer to drive in stakes
- Hammer
- Strikeoff

Creating a curb

Concrete edgings are done in a manner similar to "invisible" edgings, except that the concrete is placed higher, to be level with the masonry units. Use 2x4 lumber for the temporary form. Strike the concrete off flush *(page 74)* with the top of the form, creating a curb for the paving. You can finish the surface of the concrete in a variety of ways; see page 78.

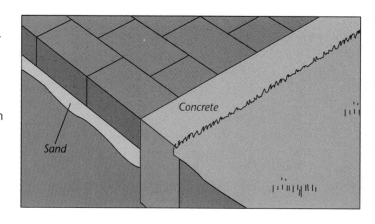

LAYING MASONRY UNITS

After you have graded the area and built the edgings, you're ready to start paving. Check the information on page 51 to make sure that you've selected a method that is suitable for the units you're using. Laying units in sand is explained below; the dry-mortar method on page 57; and the wet-mortar method on page 58. In each case, your first step will be placing and striking off a bed; next, you'll lay the units with the appropriate spacing; finally, you'll fill the joints to secure the units in place.

Laying bricks or concrete pavers in sand

TOOLKIT
• Lumber for strikeoff, or bladed strikeoff
• Tamper
• Mason's line
• Rubber mallet
• Pointing or mason's trowel
• Bench brush

1 ▶ Striking off the base
After grading the area to be paved and constructing edgings, you can begin to lay the sand base.

Set temporary guides inside the edgings, their top surfaces one brick-thickness below the finished grade. If you use 2x4s, as shown above, the sand bed will be approximately 2" deep. Place dampened sand between the guides; strike it off smooth, about 3' at a time, with a straight piece of lumber. Tamp the sand (see the tamper on page 63), then restrike as necessary. If your project is narrow enough, you can also use the bladed strikeoff *(page 19)*, resting on the edgings, instead of using the temporary guides.

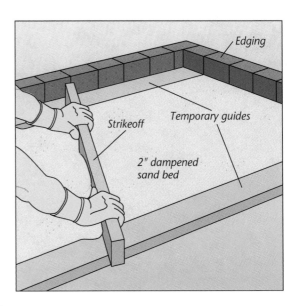

2 ▶ Setting the bricks or pavers
Working from a corner outward, place the bricks or pavers, tapping them into place with a mallet or piece of wood *(left)*. (For brick bond patterns see page 51; to see how to cut a brick, turn to page 26.) A mason's line aids alignment. Remove the temporary guides as you work, and use a trowel to fill in the area with sand. Strike off the area where the guide was with a short board. Use the leveled section as a guide, being careful not to disturb it.

3 ▶ Sanding the joints
Spread fine sand over the surface of the finished paving. Let it dry thoroughly, then sweep it into the joints, resanding as necessary to fill them. Use a fine spray to wet the finished paving down; this helps settle the sand.

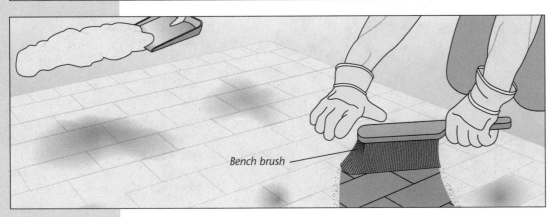

Laying other units in sand

TOOLKIT
- Lumber for strikeoff, or bladed strikeoff
- Tamper
- Mason's line
- Rubber mallet
- Pointing or mason's trowel
- Bench brush
- Hammer
- Brickset
- Saw or hatchet

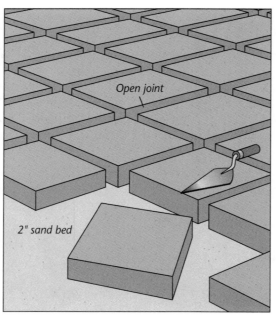

Open joint

2" sand bed

Laying adobe
Sand-bedding is best for adobe. Strike off the base, using the same 2" bed you'd use for brick. Set the adobes as you would bricks or pavers *(page 55),* but take extra care that the blocks don't straddle humps or bridge hollows; otherwise, they may crack.

Leave 1" open joints between blocks; this makes up for irregularities in block sizes and allows you to pack the joints with sand or earth and crevice planting. Running bond, jack-on-jack, and basketweave patterns *(page 51)* all work well. The latter two do not require cutting. If you need to cut an adobe block, however, it's easy to do with a hammer and brickset *(page 26),* or with an old saw or hatchet.

Laying stone
Lay stones in a 2" sand bed, following the directions for brick *(page 55);* edgings are optional. Scoop out or fill in sand as necessary to compensate for variations in stone thickness. If you're using irregularly-shaped stones, lay them out in advance, adjusting the pattern and the joint spacing as needed. Use a level as you work.

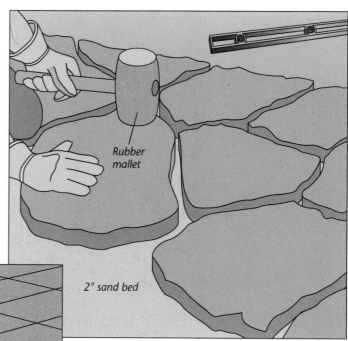

Rubber mallet

2" sand bed

Butted joint

1/2" sand bed

Laying tile
Heavy 3/4" thick tile can be laid in sand. Follow the directions for brick *(page 55),* but use a 1/2" sand base; a thicker base may allow the tiles to tilt out of position. If possible, use butted joints (tiles laid with edges touching), as these will give a little added stability.

Laying masonry units in dry mortar

TOOLKIT
- Strikeoff
- Tamper
- $1/2$" thick wooden spacer
- Mason's line
- Scrub brush
- Broom
- $1/2$" thick board for tamping joints
- Joint-striking tool

Mortar

Scrub brush

1 Placing the units and mortar
For dry-mortared brick, stone, and tile pavings, follow steps 1 and 2 on page 55, then the steps below. Don't use this method for adobe or interlocking concrete pavers. Set the units with $1/2$" open joints (use a $1/2$" thick wooden spacer and a mason's line for alignment). Mix dry cement and sand in a 1:4 ratio and spread it over the surface, brushing it into the open joints *(above)*. Kneel on a board to avoid disturbing the paving. Then, carefully sweep the mortar off the unit surfaces.

Wooden tamper

2 Tamping the mortar
Use a piece of $1/2$" thick wood to tamp the dry mix firmly into the joints: this improves the bond. Carefully sweep and dust the unit faces before going on to the next step: Any mix that remains may leave stains. (Some staining is usually unavoidable with this method.)

3 Wetting the surface
Using an extremely fine spray, so as not to splash mortar out of the joints, wet down the paving. Don't allow pools to form, and try not to wash away any of the mortar. Over the next 2 to 3 hours, wet the paving periodically, keeping it damp. Tool the joints when the mortar is firm enough *(page 31)*. After a few hours, you can scrub the unit faces with burlap to help remove mortar stains. For further cleanup instructions, turn to page 32.

TOOLKIT
- Small sledgehammer to drive stakes
- Hammer
- Wheelbarrow
- Mason's trowel or square shovel
- Bladed strikeoff
- Mason's line
- Level
- Mortar board
- Pointing trowel
- Convex jointer

1 **Preparing**

Bricks can be wet-mortared over an old concrete slab or over one you've just made *(page 70)*. Wet down your bricks several hours before you start work; this will prevent them from absorbing too much water from the mortar. Prepare the mortar using a 1:4 cement-sand mix with no lime *(page 20)*.

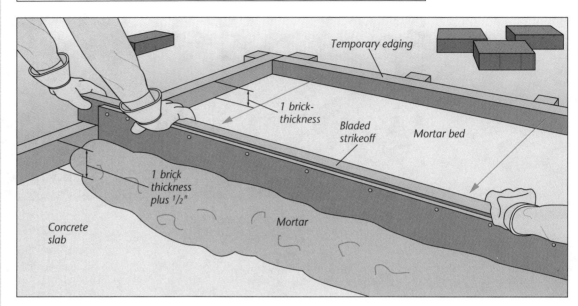

Temporary edging

1 brick-thickness

Bladed strikeoff

Mortar bed

1 brick thickness plus ¹/₂"

Concrete slab

Mortar

2 **Placing the mortar bed**

Place a ¹/₂" thick wet-mortar bed between temporary edgings staked against the slab; the edgings are set for the thickness of a brick plus ¹/₂" to allow for the mortar bed. Dump the mortar from the wheelbarrow and smooth or shovel it onto the surface with a mason's trowel or square shovel. Strike off the bed using a bladed strikeoff that rides on the edgings and extends down one brick-thickness below them. Mix only as much mortar as you can use in an hour or so, and strike off only about 10 square feet at a time. Get a helper for this step if possible.

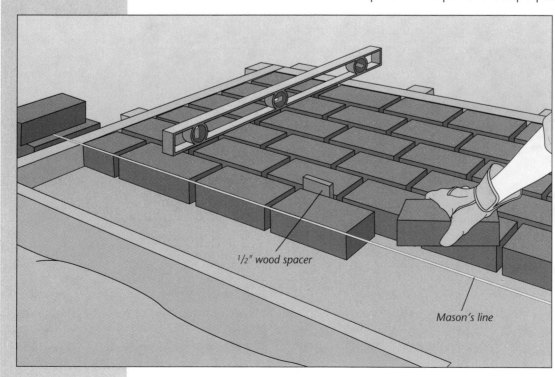

¹/₂" wood spacer

Mason's line

3 **Placing the bricks**

Place the bricks in your chosen pattern *(page 51)*, leaving ¹/₂" open joints between them (use a wood spacer). Gently tap each one to bed it. Use a mason's line and a level for alignment.

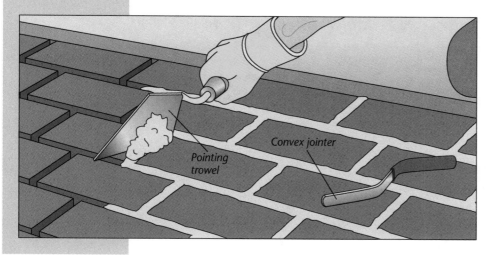

4 Filling the joints
Use a small trowel to pack mortar—the same mix as the bed—into the joints, working carefully to minimize spilling. Add lime if desired to improve the workability of the mortar. Tool the joints with a convex jointer, broom handle, or other convex object *(page 31)*. Scrub the paving several hours later with burlap to remove mortar "tags" and stains. Instructions for further cleaning are on page 32.

Pointing trowel

Convex jointer

ASK A PRO

WHAT OTHER UNITS CAN I SET IN WET MORTAR?
You can use the wet-mortar method to set tile and stone. Don't use it with adobe and interlocking concrete pavers. Adobe should always be set in sand, with large, open joints (page 54); it's not advisable to use mortar. Adobe is sturdy

stuff, but salt action that occurs at mortar joints can cause the edges of the blocks to crumble.

You can't use mortar with interlocking concrete pavers because there is no room for it in their tight-fitting joints.

Laying tiles in wet mortar

TOOLKIT
• Small sledgehammer for driving stakes
• Wheelbarrow
• Mason's trowel or square shovel
• Lumber for bladed strikeoff
• Mason's line
• Level
• Mortar board
• Coffee can
• Joint-striking tool

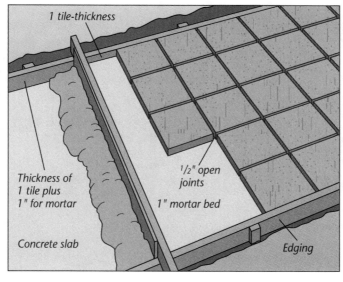

1 tile-thickness

Thickness of 1 tile plus 1" for mortar

Concrete slab

1/2" open joints

1" mortar bed

Edging

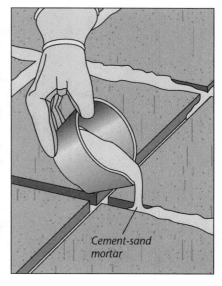

Cement-sand mortar

1 Placing the tiles
Lay the tile over a concrete slab, using the same basic method as for brick *(opposite)*. The edgings can be left in place or removed after the mortar has set. Set tile in a 1" mortar bed for better leveling and extra support. Use the same mortar mix as for brick but with less water because tile is less absorbent than brick. (For information on mixing mortar see page 20.) Use a bladed strikeoff that rides on the edgings as shown; when tiles are laid on top, they will be flush with the tops of the edgings. Use wood spacers or special plastic tile spacers to maintain 1/2" joints, removing the spacers before filling the joints.

2 Filling the joints
Wait 24 hours after setting the tiles, then fill the joints with a 1:3 cement-sand mortar mix with no lime. The mortar should be just thin enough to pour. Use a coffee can bent to form a spout to fill the joints, cleaning away spills immediately. Tool the joints as you would for brick *(page 31)*, using a pipe or convex jointer.

Tile can be laid over a wood floor, but be sure to check with your supplier to find out how much extra weight will be involved; then consult your building department to see if your floor can carry it.

The drawing at right illustrates the layered construction method—tar paper and light-gauge wire mesh are laid over the floor before the tile is set. A flexible grout is then applied.

This approach can be used either indoors or outdoors. Tile can also be applied with adhesive indoors. In this case, plywood underlayment would have to be nailed over a plank floor; tar paper and wire mesh would not be used. See your supplier or a tile setter for the method and products that suit your situation.

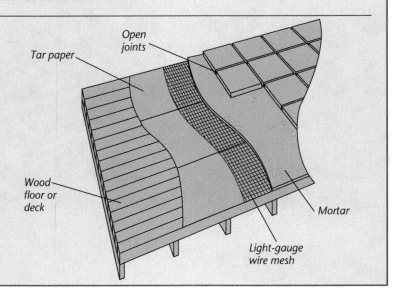

Tar paper
Open joints
Wood floor or deck
Mortar
Light-gauge wire mesh

Laying stone in wet mortar

TOOLKIT
- Mortar board
- Mason's trowel
- Level
- Straightedge
- Rubber mallet
- Pointing trowel

For trimming stone:
- Brickset or stone chisel
- Hand-drilling hammer

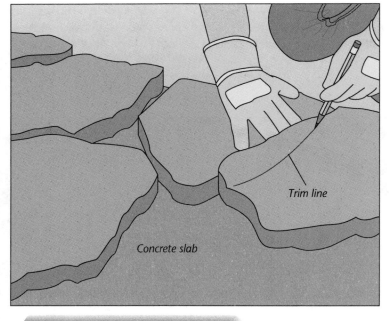

Trim line

Concrete slab

1 Preparing the site
Arrange the stones in a pleasing pattern allowing approximately the same space for mortar joints throughout. Trim stones as necessary, marking them as shown.

Mix mortar using a 1:3 cement-sand mix without lime. Stone should be set in rather stiff mortar because, like tile, it is relatively non-absorbent. For information on mixing mortar, refer to page 20.

ASK A PRO

HOW DO I TRIM STONE?
To trim a stone, lap it over its neighbor and mark the trim line (above). To cut, score the line with a brickset or stone-mason's chisel (near right), prop the edge to be cut off on a wood scrap, and strike the scored line with a brickset (or stone chisel) and a hand-drilling hammer (far right).

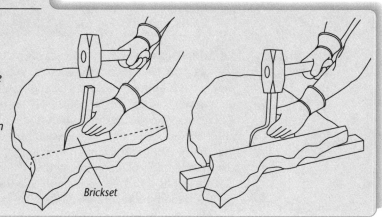

Brickset

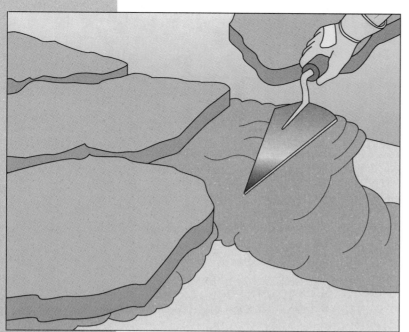

2 Setting the stones

To set stones, trowel enough mortar onto the slab to make full mortar beds for one or two stones at a time. Unless you are using sawn stone, such as slate, you'll need to vary the thickness of the setting bed to make up for variations in stone thickness, but it should be at least 1" thick. Keep the mortar stiff enough to support the stones. Make sure stones are clean and dry to be certain you're getting a good bond.

3 Bedding the stones

Set each stone firmly in place and bed it by tapping with a rubber mallet. Use a straightedge and level to maintain an even surface.

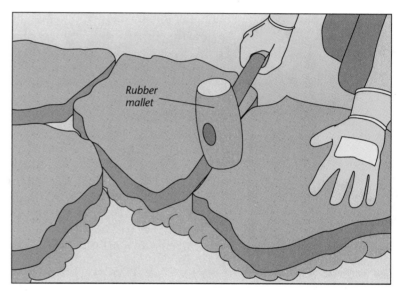

Rubber mallet

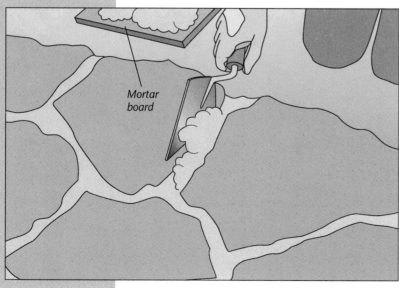

Mortar board

4 Filling the joints

Let the mortar set for 24 hours, then pack mortar between the stones. Add one-half part fireclay to the mortar if desired, to improve workability. Do not use lime; it may leave stains. Smooth the joints with a pointing trowel, and clean up spills with a sponge and water. Muriatic acid washes, commonly used to clean cured masonry, can be used except with limestone and marble; the acid mars these types of stone.

PAVING: CAST CONCRETE

Cast concrete is the modern age's answer to stone. It is integral to foundation work, and no high-rise structure could be built without it. Concrete has made possible everything from fencepost anchors to freeways. This chapter will show you how to construct a cast-concrete footing for a wall, and how to pave with concrete. (Cast-concrete walls are difficult for the beginner and will not be covered here.) You'll also learn how to buy and mix concrete, how to construct forms, how to place concrete, and how to create a variety of surfaces with cast-concrete paving.

If you work with masonry, you'll need to work with concrete, if only to get your project—literally—off the ground. A strong concrete footing is basic to most masonry walls whether they're built of units *(page 17)* or cast in place. Steel reinforcement increases tensile strength of footings, and keeps cracks from widening.

By itself, concrete can also create attractive, durable paving. Using cast concrete as paving means you can create anything from small stepping-stones to sizable slabs. The surface can be made smooth enough for shuffleboard, or rough enough to keep you from slipping on a steep pathway. Concrete can be colored, embedded with attractive stones, or made to resemble stone itself.

Note that in this chapter we will use the terms "cast" and "place" instead of the terms "poured" and "pour" when referring to concrete, as well as the term "plastic concrete" instead of "wet concrete."

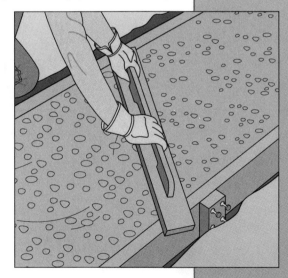

A concrete pavement doesn't have to be plain. Many interesting finishes are possible. Shown here is aggregate being embedded in the surface with a darby.

BEFORE YOU BEGIN

Once you've decided to work with concrete, you'll need to decide how to buy the concrete, and how to have it delivered. For a concrete formula and information on how much of each ingredient you'll need for your job, see page 64. Instructions on mixing concrete begin on page 65.

Special concrete masonry tools are shown below; only the magnesium hand float, jointer, and edger need to be purchased. Garden tools will do in most cases, and wooden floats can be homemade. You may also need the mason's level, mason's trowel, and mortar box shown on page 19.

When working with concrete, proper safety equipment is required. Everyone on the job should wear safety goggles. Wear long sleeves and pants and water-resistant work gloves. Spills on skin and clothing should be rinsed off immediately. And, if your hands feel rough and dry after finishing a job, wash them and then apply lanolin hand cream. A case of severe skin discomfort needs a doctor's attention. For information on safety equipment, turn to page 18.

BUYING CONCRETE

Here you have several choices to make. Depending upon how much personal involvement you want, you can make up your own mix from scratch, buy dry prepackaged mix, haul your own plastic (wet) mix, or have ready-mix delivered by truck.

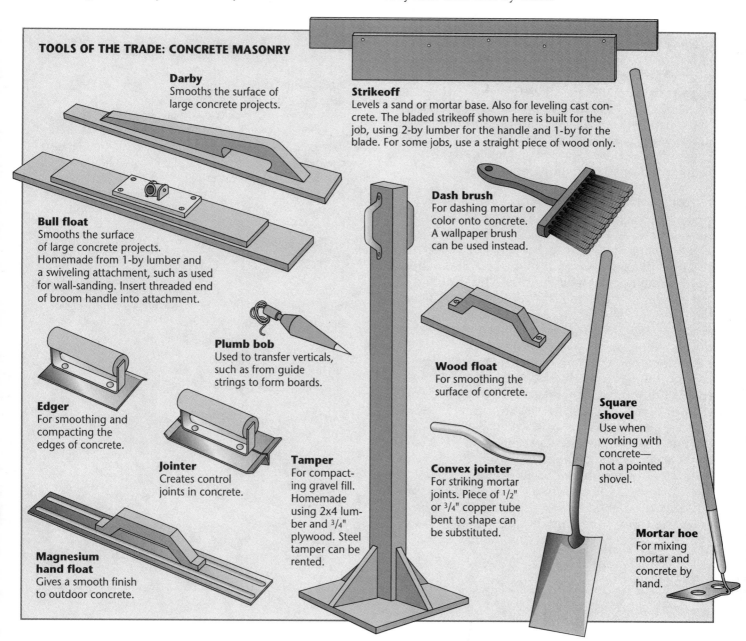

TOOLS OF THE TRADE: CONCRETE MASONRY

Darby
Smooths the surface of large concrete projects.

Strikeoff
Levels a sand or mortar base. Also for leveling cast concrete. The bladed strikeoff shown here is built for the job, using 2-by lumber for the handle and 1-by for the blade. For some jobs, use a straight piece of wood only.

Bull float
Smooths the surface of large concrete projects. Homemade from 1-by lumber and a swiveling attachment, such as used for wall-sanding. Insert threaded end of broom handle into attachment.

Dash brush
For dashing mortar or color onto concrete. A wallpaper brush can be used instead.

Plumb bob
Used to transfer verticals, such as from guide strings to form boards.

Wood float
For smoothing the surface of concrete.

Edger
For smoothing and compacting the edges of concrete.

Jointer
Creates control joints in concrete.

Tamper
For compacting gravel fill. Homemade using 2x4 lumber and 3/4" plywood. Steel tamper can be rented.

Convex jointer
For striking mortar joints. Piece of 1/2" or 3/4" copper tube bent to shape can be substituted.

Square shovel
Use when working with concrete—not a pointed shovel.

Magnesium hand float
Gives a smooth finish to outdoor concrete.

Mortar hoe
For mixing mortar and concrete by hand.

Bulk dry materials: You usually save money by ordering your materials and doing your own mixing. For small projects, though, surcharges for small-quantity delivery can eat up your savings, so check carefully before ordering, and explore the alternatives. The most economical method is to haul the materials yourself.

Dry pre-packaged mix: Bagged, dry, concrete mix is hard to beat for convenience. Though it is a very expensive way of buying concrete, it can be the most economical on small jobs; simply add water yourself.

Haul-it-yourself plastic mix: Some dealers supply trailers containing concrete with the water already added. These carry about 1 cubic yard of concrete; you haul it yourself with your car. The trailer may have a revolving drum to mix the concrete as you go, or it may be a simple metal or fiberglass box into which the plastic concrete is placed. A word of caution: These trailers are very heavy; be sure your tires and brakes are in good shape and that your vehicle and trailer hitch are rated for the weight.

Ready-mix: A commercial ready-mix truck is the best choice for large-scale work. The truck can deliver a large quantity all at once, so you can finish big projects in a single placement. Locate concrete plants in the Yellow Pages; many have minimum orders, so be sure to check.

A concrete pumping contractor can supply special equipment to reach awkward spots. The pump forces ready-mixed concrete through a large hose that can be run over fences and around houses.

CHOOSING A METHOD OF DELIVERY AND PLACEMENT

If possible, the placement of the concrete should be done all at once. If it is to be done in stages, you should plan to complete separate sections in single placements. (A single placement may require several batches of plastic concrete, but a batch should not be allowed to dry before the next one is placed.) Never interrupt a placement once it has begun, and remember that hot, dry weather will substantially shorten your available working time.

Forms can be filled from a wheelbarrow—you can either dump (you might need a ramp) or shovel. Or you can dump the concrete directly from the drum of a power mixer placed next to the form.

Unless your job is very small, you may need some help when it comes to the actual placement of the concrete. If you're doing your own mixing, you'll find it helpful to have one person mixing while others wheel and place the concrete. If you call for a ready-mix truck, you'll certainly need extra hands, especially if you have to move the concrete any distance, such as from the truck to the backyard.

A CONCRETE FORMULA

For most residential footing and paving projects, the concrete formula that follows will give good results. You'll need to choose between the basic mix and one containing an air-entraining agent.

Basic concrete: Use this formula for regular concrete. All proportions are by volume and are based on the use of $3/4$ inch coarse aggregate (stone).
- 1 part portland cement
- $2^1/_2$ parts sand
- $2^1/_2$ parts stone or gravel aggregate
- $1/_2$ part water

The sand should be clean concrete sand (never use beach sand); the gravel should range from quite small to about $3/4$ inch in size. The water should be drinkable—neither excessively alkaline nor acidic, nor containing organic matter.

Air-entrained concrete: Adding an air-entraining agent to the concrete mix creates tiny air bubbles in the finished concrete. These help it to expand and contract without cracking, a quality important in areas with cycles of freezing and thawing. The agent also makes concrete more workable and easier to place—the extra workability means you can add less water to a batch. This makes the finished concrete stronger. An air-entraining agent should be added to ready-mix, whatever the local climate. Specify this when you place your order.

The amount of agent you'll need to add will vary by brand, so consult your supplier. If you're using an air-entraining agent, reduce the sand to $2^1/_4$ parts.

To know how much concrete to buy, refer to the table below. The figures given are for 10 cubic feet of finished concrete and include 10% extra for waste. You don't want to run out, and you can always use any leftovers for stepping-stones (page 82) or other small projects. Note that the final volume is less than the sum of the ingredients because the smaller particles fit in among the larger ones. If you order bulk materials sold by the cubic yard, remember that each cubic yard contains 27 cubic feet.

INGREDIENTS FOR 10 CUBIC FEET OF CONCRETE

Bulk dry materiel	Portland cement: 2.6 sacks Sand: 5.8 cubic feet Gravel: 6.5 cubic feet
Dry pre-packaged mix	20 60–pound bags
Ready-mix	.41 cubic yards

SHOULD I MIX MY CONCRETE BY HAND OR MACHINE?

If your project is small, mixing the concrete by hand is undoubtedly the simplest method. However, for large forms that must be filled in a single placement, the use of a power mixer may be warranted.

Generally, any mixer that is smaller than 3 cubic feet is more nuisance than it's worth, and a mortar box (page 19) is a much better bet. A small mortar box (11x25x53 inches)

will readily take up to 2 cubic feet of concrete—a half sack of cement—at a time. Note that if you're using air-entrained concrete, you will have to choose a power mixer. Hand mixing is simply not vigorous enough to create the air bubbles you need in the concrete mix.

Whichever method you choose, make sure that you add the water in small amounts; too much can ruin the mix.

Mixing concrete by hand

TOOLKiT

- Wheelbarrow for small batches; mortar box or wooden platform for large batches
- Square shovel or 1-cubic-foot box
- Mortar hoe

Using a mortar hoe

A high-sided contractor's wheelbarrow with pneumatic tires is suitable for mixing if you don't need to work more than 1 to 2 cubic feet at a time. You can also use a large piece of plywood or a mortar box, either one homemade of plywood or a ready-made model available at masonry supply stores. Plan to work in small batches; this will make mixing easier and give you greater control over proportions.

Ingredients for small quantities of concrete are usually measured with a shovel—it's accurate enough if your scoopfuls are consistent. Use a container of known volume to measure the approximate volume of a shovelful. If you need greater accuracy you can use a 1-cubic-foot wooden box (make it bottomless for easy dumping—lifting the box empties the contents). Or, empty half a sack of

cement into a large bucket, then level and mark the bucket; this equals $1/2$ cubic foot.

Mark another bucket off in quarts and gallons to keep track of the water. And set up so that you can bail water from a drum or garbage can; it's more convenient than turning a hose on and off.

To mix concrete, place the sand on the mixing surface and add the cement, mixing thoroughly; add the gravel and mix again. Next, mound up the mixture and hollow out the center, and using the marked bucket, pour in the water. Work around the hollow, pulling the dry ingredients into the water, always enlarging the size of the basin. Continue mixing until the concrete is all the same color and all dry ingredients are damp. This makes a small trial batch, allowing you to check and adjust proportions as explained on page 66.

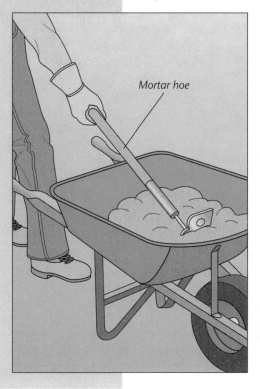

Mortar hoe

Plywood platform

Mortar box

Mixing concrete by machine

TOOLKIT
• Square shovel

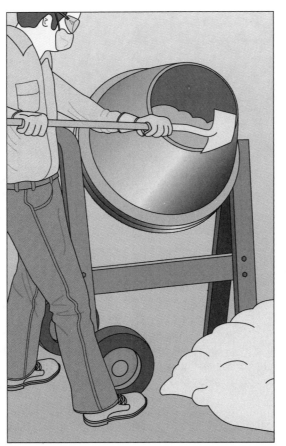

Using a concrete mixer

You can rent, borrow, or buy concrete mixers in sizes ranging from $1/2$ to 7 cubic foot capacity, but the smaller ones (under 3 cubic feet) don't pay off. A mixer can be either electric or gas-powered. Set the mixer close to your sand and gravel piles so that you can shovelfeed directly; be sure the mixer is level, and chock (wedge) it in place to prevent "walking." Concrete mixers can be dangerous; be sure to read the safety information below.

To mix ingredients, add half the water and all the coarse aggregate with the mixer off. Then, turn it on (warm it up if it's a gas one) to scour the drum. Follow with all of the sand, along with all but the last 10% of the water. Next, add the portland cement. When the mixture is a uniform color and texture, add the rest of the water and the air-entraining agent if you're using it. After adding the final ingredients, mix for at least 2 minutes; continue for longer if necessary to get a uniform appearance. Measure your ingredients by equal shovelfuls as you add them. Always throw the ingredients from outside the rotating drum.

 PLAY IT SAFE

WORKING WITH A CONCRETE MIXER

Be sure to follow all safety measures recommended for the concrete mixer you are using. Never reach into a rotating mixer drum with your hands or tools. Wear tight clothes, a dust mask, and goggles, and keep well away from the moving parts. Do not look into the mixer while running—check the mix by dumping a little out.

To avoid shock hazard, an electric mixer must be plugged into a ground-fault circuit-interrupter (GFCI) outlet. It needs a three-prong grounding-type plug and outdoor-rated three-wire extension cord. Do not run an electric

mixer in wet or damp conditions and be sure to cover it with a tarpaulin when not in use.

The engine on a gasoline-powered mixer should be fueled from a proper can for storing and pouring flammable fuel. Add fuel only when the engine has been stopped and has cooled off. Any fuel spills should be wiped up immediately. Close the fuel container tightly after fueling. While the engine is running, don't work or stand where you must breathe the exhaust fumes. And don't run the mixer in an enclosed space.

Making a trial batch

TOOLKIT
• Mason's trowel

Testing the consistency of the concrete mixture

Work a sample of your first batch with a mason's trowel. The concrete should slide—not run—freely off the trowel. You should be able to smooth the surface fairly easily, so that the large aggregate is submerged. All of the large and small aggregate at the edges of the sample should be completely and evenly coated with cement.

If your mix is too stiff and crumbly, add a little water. If it's too wet and soupy, add some sand-cement mixture. Be sure the sand and cement are correctly proportioned according to your recipe. If you do make adjustments to the recipe, be sure to record them accurately for the next batch.

BUILDING CONCRETE FOOTINGS

No matter what type of masonry material you're using for your wall, concrete is the material of choice for the footing. Local codes usually specify that the bottom of the footing be below the frost line. In some areas, this may mean starting as much as 4 feet below ground. If the footing is 8 inches thick, its top clearly will also be below ground as will the bottom section of the wall itself. Our illustrations are based on the requirements of a non-frost region, where the top of the footing can be flush with the ground. Be sure to check the code for your area. Typical footings are twice the width of the wall and equal in depth to the width *(page 22)*, but be sure to consult local building codes for exceptions to this rule of thumb. The footing should be flat on top if a unit masonry wall is to be built on top of it.

Forms for footings: Forms are the the wooden structures that hold and mold the plastic concrete to create your footing or wall. Building forms is not difficult, but it is exacting. Concrete is dense and heavy; it exerts a lot of pressure on the forms, so they must be very sturdy. The instructions below give a standard method of building forms. There are many others.

Steel reinforcing: Like other masonry materials, concrete is enormously strong in compression. A concrete column can resist crushing forces of thousands of pounds per square inch. But if a rod or chain were made of concrete, it would snap before it could lift a fraction of the weight it supported in compression. The force that snaps it is tension.

Steel changes all this; placing steel rods where tension forces concentrate enables concrete to resist the tension. Local codes specify exactly how much and what kind of reinforcing you'll need; for this reason, we cannot specify details here.

ASK A PRO

WHAT IS HYDRATION?
Hydration, a process whereby cement and water combine chemically, is the key to hardness in finished concrete. Some care must be taken to ensure that this process proceeds slowly and completely; if water is allowed to evaporate too quickly from concrete, hydration will be incomplete, and the *finished concrete will be weak. To ensure that hydration will be complete, damp-curing is used. With a concrete slab, this is accomplished by covering the freshly placed slab with a plastic sheet or a spray-on curing film, or simply by keeping it wet for several days.*

Making a footing

TOOLKIT
- Tape measure
- Saw
- Hammer
- Small sledge-hammer
- Pointed shovel for digging
- Square shovel for concrete
- Tamper (optional)
- Lumber for strikeoff

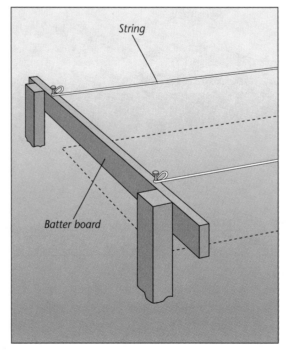

String

Batter board

1 Laying out the footing and preparing the base
Use strings and batter boards as a guide for the footing trench. To construct the batter board, drive in 2x2 stakes with a small sledge-hammer at each end of the trench and nail on 2x4s at least as wide as the trench. (Make the trench about 1" wider and longer than the finished slab will be.) Attach strings to mark the edges of the trench *(left)*. You can also use these strings as guides for your forms once the trench is complete.

Because concrete needs uniform support, it should never be cast on backfilled soil. For this reason, the bottom of the trench is excavated to the correct depth. If you should happen to dig too deep, let concrete fill the excess—do not backfill. If the soil is soft, dig it out and replace it with well-tamped gravel.

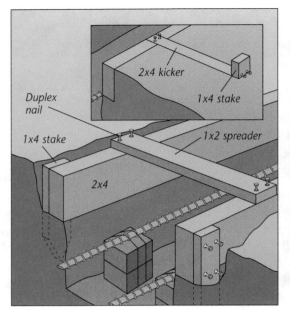

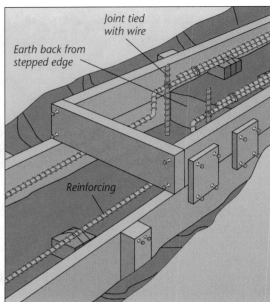

2 Constructing a form

The easiest route to a footing is simply to dig a trench and cast concrete in the earth. In cases where the earth is too soft or too damp to hold a vertical edge, you can build a simple form, as shown above left, using the batter board strings as a guide. Build the form from 2x4s. Both sides should be level across. Stake the side forms with 1x4 or 2x2 wood stakes no more than 4' apart. Use 3½" duplex nails (for easy removal) in 2" lumber or 2½" nails in 1" lumber. Spreaders made of 1x2 wood can be nailed to the tops of the forms to keep them properly separated until the concrete is placed, then the spreaders are removed for striking.

If the earth is difficult to stake, shorter stakes can be placed a foot or two back from the edge of the trench instead and the forms held by 2x4 kickers reaching back to them, sunk in a shallow trench (inset). In very sandy soil, you may need to build the form from 2x8 wood that extends all the way to the bottom of the trench.

Steel reinforcing can be supported on pieces of brick, stone, or broken concrete. It should be placed one half of the footing's thickness up from the bottom of the trench.

If you are building on a sloping site, plan to use a stepped footing (above, right).

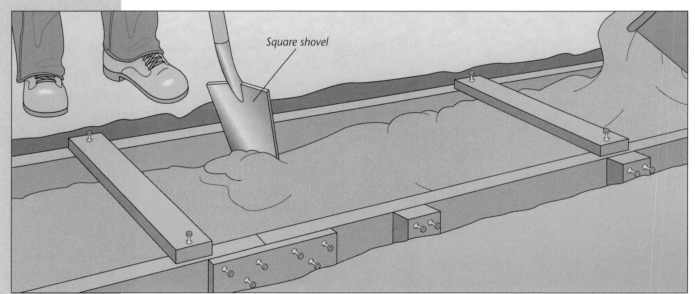

3 Placing the concrete

Coat the insides of the form with form-release agent so it can later be separated from the concrete and removed. Then, place the concrete for the footing, compacting it firmly with a shovel.

Run the shovel up and down along the edges of the forms to ensure that no voids are left. In placement and compacting, always work systematically from one end of the footing to the other.

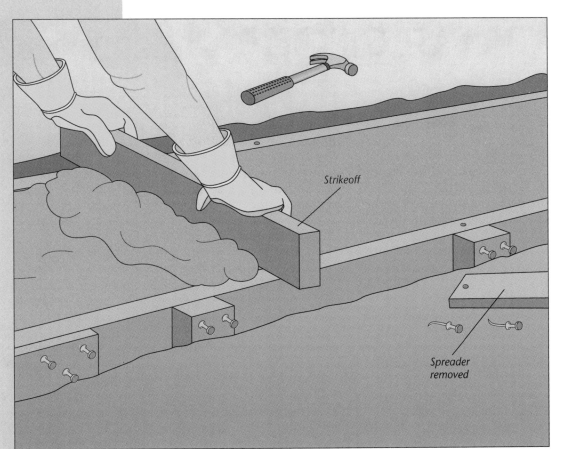

◀ **4** **Striking off**
First, remove the spreaders. Use a piece of wood to strike the concrete level with the top of the form. Work with a zigzag motion from one end to the other, knocking down high spots and filling any hollows.

Strikeoff

Spreader removed

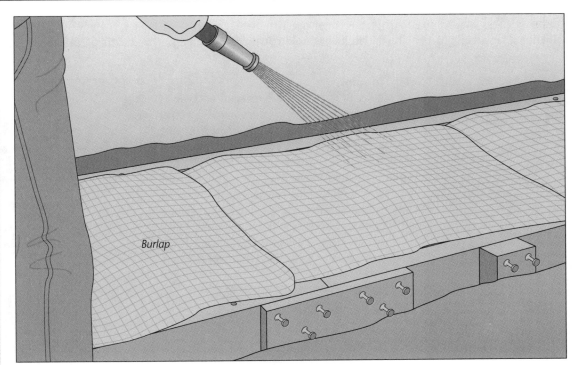

Burlap

5 **Curing the concrete**
After striking, the footing should be cured for 7 days; the longer the cure, the stronger the concrete. Cover it with burlap, damp sand, plastic sheeting, or a spray-on curing compound available from your masonry supplier. Keep the porous coverings wet to ensure hydration: Spray them several times a day with a hose, especially if the weather is hot and dry. Once curing is complete, remove the forms.

PAVING WITH CAST CONCRETE

In this section you'll learn how to pave with concrete—how to build forms, and cast and finish the concrete. For information on ordering and mixing concrete, refer to pages 63 to 66.

Before you begin: Divide your work into stages that you and one or two other people can handle. Place large areas in sections, or cast a few paving stones at a time. As always with construction projects around the home, check with your building department about code restrictions that may apply to your project. A garden path will likely be no problem, but a major patio project might. You'll need to take into account the soil, drainage, and frost conditions for your area; local building officials can be a real help here.

Once concrete is in place, you're stuck with it; repair and replacement are costly. Take your time in planning and preparation, and be sure the site is ready. Concrete requires a stable, well-drained base that gives it uniform support. Because the finished slab is monolithic, it's especially important to ensure that the ground beneath it doesn't shift and cause the concrete to crack.

The standard slab for pathways and patios is 4 inches thick, with a slight pitch for water runoff. Usually 2x4s are used for forms in concrete paving work, so that actual thickness would be 3½ inches if you use finished lumber. For a slab of the right thickness, use rough, undressed lumber, which has slightly larger dimensions, or dig ½ inch below the forms for a thicker slab. Lumber can be left in place as permanent edgings and dividers; in this case, be sure to use redwood or cedar. Get heartwood if you can, and, unless you're using redwood or cedar, be sure to treat the wood with a preservative before committing it to the earth. Pressure-treated lumber rated for ground contact is also a good choice. Instructions begin on page 71 for building straight, stepped, and curved forms.

Jointing a slab: A concrete slab needs two kinds of joints: control joints and isolation joints. Control joints are tooled into the plastic concrete with a jointer during finishing. They provide hidden places for the slab to crack as it shrinks on hardening. Leave-in forms also serve as control joints. Do not use control joints, however, if mortared-in-place pavers such as brick or tile are to be placed atop the slab. In this case, use heavy wire mesh to hold the concrete together *(page 73)*.

Use isolation joints wherever a new slab adjoins previous construction, as where a patio meets a driveway or the house foundation. They allow independent movement of the structures. From a dealer, buy special ½-inch-thick 4-inch-wide asphalt-impregnated isolation-joint strips in 8 or 10 foot lengths and put in place before casting concrete against them.

Preparing the base

TOOLKIT
- Pointed shovel
- Stock for template
- Tape measure
- Hammer

1 ▶ Digging
Refer to page 52 for directions on laying out and grading the site for your paving. Plan on at least a 4" to 6" gravel base in areas where frost and drainage are problems. Do not cast concrete on topsoil, sod, wood, soft soil, or large rocks.

Using a pointed shovel *(right)*, cut and remove the turf to the required depth so that the slab can be cast on unexcavated soil. If a gravel bed is to be used, include its thickness in the total depth. Make the trench about a foot wider and longer than the finished slab is to be to allow room for forming.

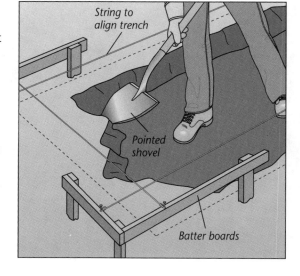

String to align trench

Pointed shovel

Batter boards

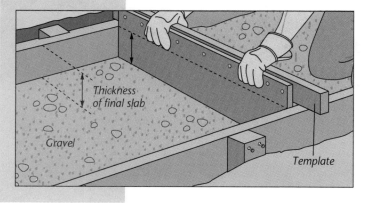

Thickness of final slab

Gravel

Template

◀ 2 Leveling a gravel base
Once the excavation is complete, build and place the forms *(page 71)*, and add the gravel, if used. It's easier to level the gravel if the forms are in place—you can use them as a guide for a template *(left)*. Spread the gravel with a shovel to the depth of the template. Allow the gravel to extend under the form to the edges of the excavation.

Building a straight form

TOOLKIT
- Tape measure
- Small sledge-hammer
- Plumb bob
- Hammer
- Level
- Saw

Assembling the form

Straight forms are the easiest to build. They can be assembled from standard lumber, either cut to length or spliced (right, above). Be sure to allow for drainage, as shown below.

When placing the form boards, nail them to sturdy 1x4 or 2x2 stakes driven into the ground at least every 4', using $3^{1}/_{2}$" nails for 2" stakes and $2^{1}/_{2}$" nails for 1" stakes. Use taut strings attached to the batter boards as guidelines. Drive the stakes plumb and deep enough so that they will not over-lap the top of the form and obstruct the strikeoff, or cut them off flush with the forms. Use the batter boards and strings to lay out accurate corners. Nail the corners securely, and stake them well. The plastic concrete will exert considerable pressure on the form, so be sure your stakes are secure. Don't forget to space them the thickness of the form boards out from the edge of the finished slab; for 2x4s, this would be $1^{1}/_{2}$".

When nailing a leave-in form board to a stake, and to assemble the form, use galvanized nails. Also, drive $3^{1}/_{2}$" galvanized nails part-way into the form about every 16" on the inside; this will lock the boards to the slab (right, below). Use a sledge-hammer, or other heavy object to back up the board when nailing. Cut off the top of leave-in stakes at 45°. If you plan to strip the form, use duplex nails, as shown, to make disassembly easier.

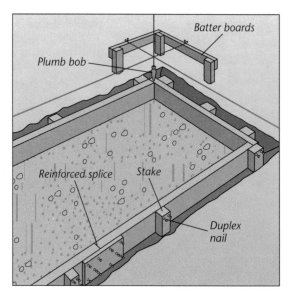

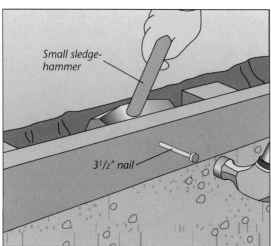

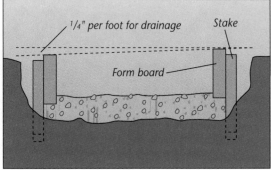

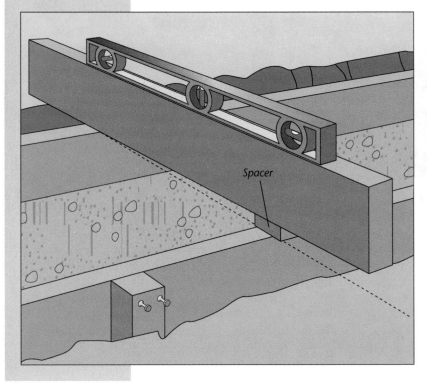

Allowing for drainage

Check the pitch of the form from side to side by placing a level on a long, straight board extending the width of the form; a spacer should be required at one end to level the board (left). Your finished slab should have at least enough pitch in one direction to allow water to run off. If the natural grade of your site isn't enough, plan to pitch the slab about $1/4$" per foot (above). Do this by nailing one sideboard slightly higher than its mate.

Building a stepped form

TOOLKIT
- Pointed shovel
- Tamper
- Tape measure
- Small sledge-hammer
- Saw
- Hammer
- Level

Digging and filling

Pathways on steeper grades are much easier to climb if they are cast in a stepped form. Each extended step can have its own pitch so that the path generally follows the natural slope of the hill.

In excavating for a stepped form, you'll probably have to do some cutting and filling. Use gravel as fill; be sure to tamp thoroughly any fill you make—it is an area where settling trouble may occur later.

When you lay in the gravel base, keep it back from the actual step area so that the concrete will be extra thick at this potentially weak point. For the nailing technique, see page 71. Check the forms for level; use a board to straddle both sides of the form *(right)*, if your level isn't long enough.

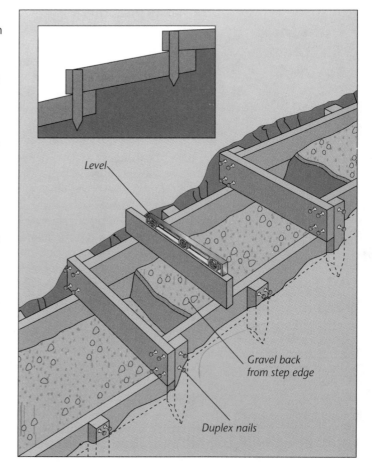

Level

Gravel back from step edge

Duplex nails

Building a curved form

- String compass
- Small sledge-hammer
- Hammer
- Circular saw or handsaw for kerfing
- Tape measure

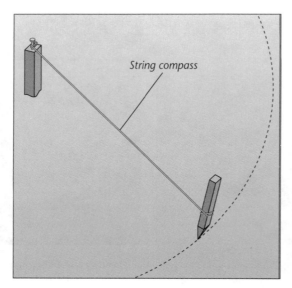

String compass

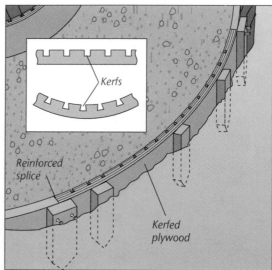

Kerfs

Reinforced splice

Kerfed plywood

Bending or saw-kerfing the form

Bending works best for gentle curves. Use plywood, with the outer grain running up and down, and bend it around stakes set on the inside edge of the curve. Determine the radius with a string compass *(above, left)*; dig the pointed end of the stick into the ground to mark the curve.

For the outside edge of the curve, bend the plywood around temporary stakes and secure the ends by nailing them to stakes set on the outside. Add more stakes on the outside, nailing the plywood to them; then pull up the inside stakes. If the plywood won't bend without breaking, use a circular saw or handsaw to kerf it *(above, right)*. For information on nailing, turn to page 71.

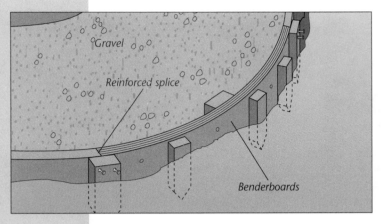
Gravel

Reinforced splice

Benderboards

Laminating the form board

Use the laminating method if the form is to remain in place. Bend several layers of benderboard (thin, rot-resistant boards—usually redwood or cedar) around the stakes until you have a thickness equal to the other form boards. Drive in some nails to keep the layers together. Add an inside stake, as shown, and then pull it up as the concrete is cast.

ASK A PRO

HOW DO I FORM REALLY TIGHT CURVES?

Really tight curves can be made only with sheet metal, plastic, or other thin, flexible material. Cut the material to size and nail it to the stakes. You may need extra stakes to ensure adequate support.

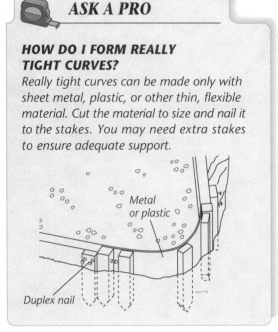

Metal or plastic

Duplex nail

Casting the concrete

TOOLKIT

- Bolt cutters or heavy pliers
- Level
- Ball-peen hammer for isolation joints
- Square shovels
- Mortar hoes
- Stock for strikeoff
- Darby or bull float
- Mason's trowel
- Edger
- Jointer (1" deep)
- Wood float or magnesium hand float
- Steel trowel (optional)

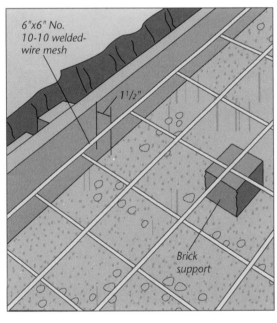

6"x6" No. 10-10 welded-wire mesh

1½"

Brick support

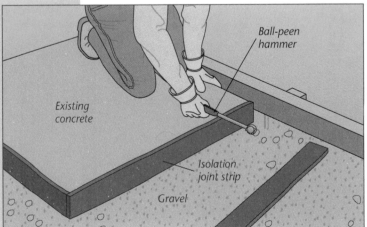

Ball-peen hammer

Existing concrete

Isolation joint strip

Gravel

1 Preparing for the casting

It's a good idea to reinforce concrete if you are not going to be able to use control joints, such as in the case of a slab that is going to be topped with mortared paving units. Steel holds the pieces together if cracking occurs. Six-inch-square No. 10-10 welded-wire mesh is most commonly used. Install the mesh after the forms are ready; cut it to size with bolt cutters or heavy pliers, keeping it at least 1½" away from the sides of the forms. Support the mesh on small stones, bits of brick, or broken concrete so that it will be held midway in the slab.

Just before placing the concrete, go over your forms to check for level (or grade) and to be sure everything is secure. Temporary forms should be coated with form-release agent to aid in stripping.

This is also the time to install isolation joints *(page 70)*, if required. Attach isolation joint strips flush with the top of concrete that is already in place. Fasten them with hardened concrete nails or construction adhesive *(left, below)*.

Before you begin, be sure you have enough hands for the job. Except for small projects, at least two people will be needed for most concrete work; remember that once the casting begins, it should proceed right through to the final curing step without interruption.

Don't neglect your tools, either. Be sure you have enough square shovels and mortar hoes to spread and compact the concrete.

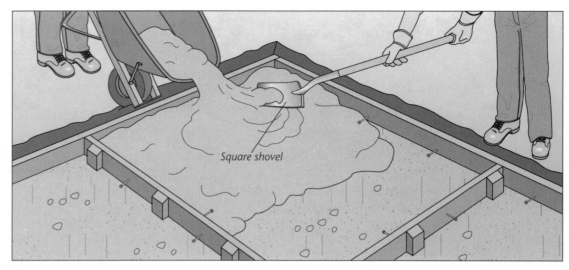

2 Placing the concrete

Thoroughly dampen the soil or gravel. Start placing the concrete at one corner of the form while a helper uses a shovel or hoe to spread it *(above)*. Work the concrete up against the form and compact it into all corners with a square shovel or mortar hoe; with a hoe, push—don't drag—the concrete. But don't overwork the concrete, and don't spread it too far; overworking will force the heavy aggregate to the bottom of slab and will bring up small particles that can cause defects in the finished concrete. Instead, space out your placement along the form, working each batch just enough to completely fill the form.

If you plan to leave in dividers, as shown, remove the inside stakes after placing the neighboring section. Don't nail them to the form.

3 Striking the concrete

Move a strikeoff (in this case a straight 2x4) across the form to level the concrete. On large jobs, do this batch-by-batch, rather than after all the concrete is placed. Move the board slowly along the form, using a zigzag, sawing motion; make 2 passes. Even on narrow forms, two people will make the work faster and more accurate. A third person can shovel extra concrete into any hollows *(left)*.

 PLAY IT SAFE

WORKING WITH CONCRETE
Always wear safety goggles when working with concrete. Plastic concrete is caustic, so wear gloves to protect your hands. Also wear rubber boots if you're going to have to walk in the concrete to strike it off. If plastic concrete comes in contact with your skin—including through clothing—wash thoroughly with water.

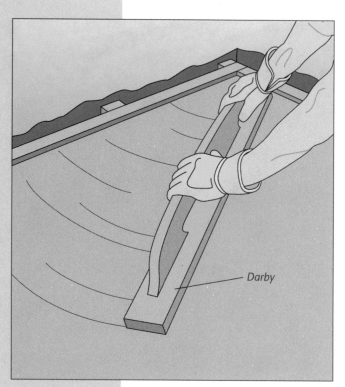

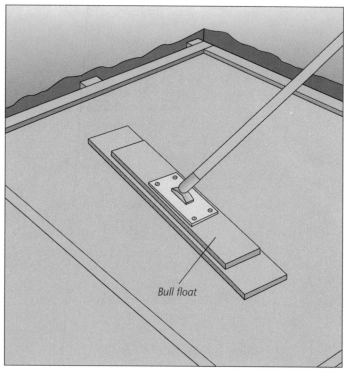

Darby

Bull float

4 Initial smoothing

(On very small projects, you can skip this step.) After striking off, use a darby or bull float—depending on the size of your project—for the initial finishing. Smooth down high spots and fill small hollows left after striking off. Use the darby *(above, left)* on small projects; move it in overlapping arcs, then repeat with overlapping straight, side-to-side strokes. Keep the tool flat, but don't let it dig in. For larger jobs, use a bull float *(above, right)*. Push it away from you with its leading edge raised slightly. Pull it back nearly flat; overlap your passes.

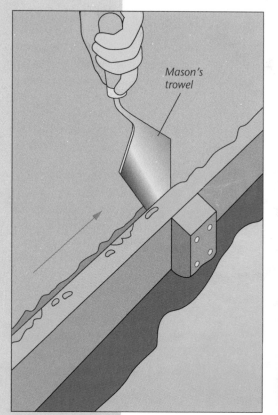

Mason's trowel

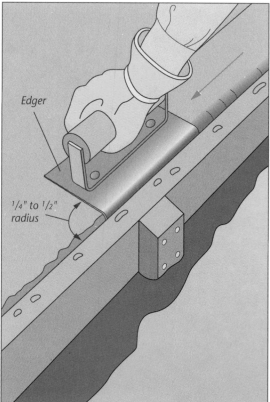

Edger

¹/₄" to ¹/₂" radius

5 Edging

To edge the concrete, begin by running a mason's trowel between the concrete and the form *(far left)*. Follow up with an edger *(near left)*. Run the tool back and forth to smooth and compact the concrete, creating a smoothly curved edge that will resist chipping.

6 ▸ Jointing

Use a 1" deep jointer with a straight guide board, as shown, to make control joints. (You can also kneel on this board if you're jointing a wide slab.) To accomplish their job, control joints need to be one quarter as deep as the slab is thick. Control joints should divide the slab into roughly square sections. Generally control joints can be made at intervals of about 1½ times the width of the slab. However, the distance between control joints should not exceed 30 times the thickness of the slab—10' apart for a 4" slab. However, if small ³⁄₄" coarse aggregate is used in the mix, it's better to reduce the maximum control-joint spacing to 8' for a 4" slab. Jointed sections should be as square as possible, never more than 1½ times as long as they are wide. Measure for the joints and use a pencil to indicate them on top of the forms.

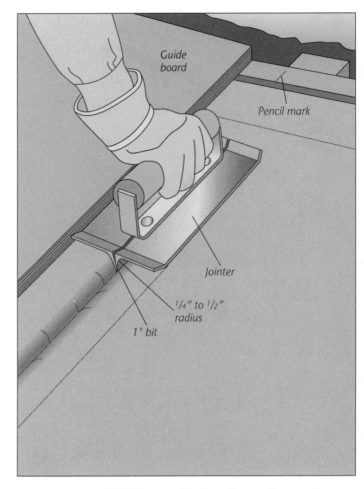

Guide board

Pencil mark

Jointer

¼" to ½" radius

1" bit

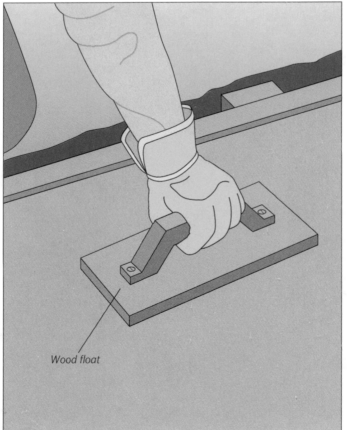

Wood float

7 Floating and troweling

After the water sheen has disappeared from the concrete, but before the surface has become really stiff, float with a wood float or a magnesium hand float. The latter gives a smoother surface, and should always be used with air-entrained concrete; a wood float can tear the surface. The leading edge of a wood or magnesium float should be raised slightly.

For a slick, smooth, indoor surface, follow the wood float with a steel trowel instead. Make your initial passes with the trowel flat on the surface; use some pressure but don't let the blade dig in. If you want a smoother surface, wait a few minutes and repeat the operation, this time with more pressure and with the leading edge slightly raised.

Kneel on boards to reach the center of a large slab; then finish over the board marks.

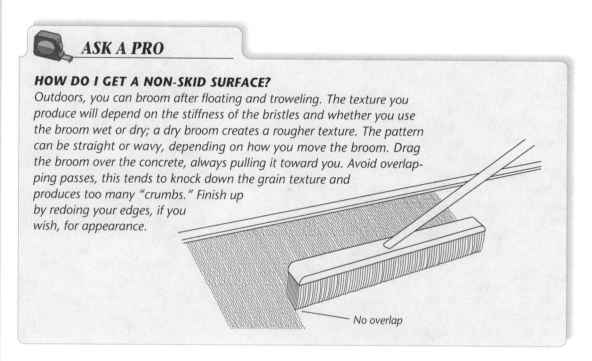
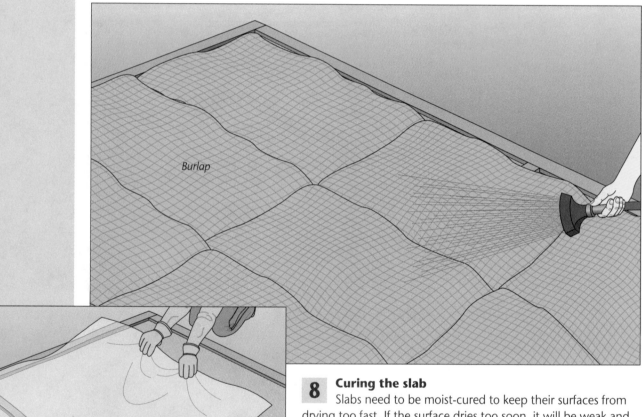

Burlap

Sheet plastic

8 Curing the slab

Slabs need to be moist-cured to keep their surfaces from drying too fast. If the surface dries too soon, it will be weak and may later become powdery or crumble away. Cure your concrete by keeping it wet. Cover the slab with burlap, sand, straw, or other material and wet it *(above)*. If you use plastic sheeting or a commercial curing compound, water evaporating from the concrete will be trapped, eliminating the need for wetting. If no covering material is available, you'll need to keep the surface damp by sprinkling with a sprinkler or a soaker hose. Curing should last at least 3 days—longer in cold weather; it's a good idea to cure your project for a week, just to be on the safe side.

GIVING A SPECIAL FINISH TO THE PAVING

The appearance of a concrete surface can be altered to suit a variety of purposes—and tastes. Here are some of the most widely used methods. (Turn to page 15 to see how some of the final surfaces look.)

Exposed aggregate: The attractive exposed aggregate finish is probably the most popular for residential concrete work. There are two ways to produce it: seeding a special aggregate or large varicolored smooth pebbles into the concrete surface (below), or exposing the regular sharp aggregate already contained in the concrete.

To expose the regular aggregate, cast and finish the concrete through the floating stage (page 73). Don't overfloat, or you may force the aggregate too deep. Then follow step 4 (opposite page). You'll get better results if you use an attractive, coarse aggregate.

Salt finish: Coarse rock salt can be used for a distinctive pocked surface on concrete (page 80). This finish is not recommended for areas with severe freezing weath-er; water trapped in the pockets will expand upon freezing, and may crack or chip the surface.

Travertine finish: For a marbled effect, try the travertine finish (page 80). Like salt finish, this finish is not resistant to severe freezing weather.

Simulated flagstones: One way to break up a dull expanse of plain concrete is to tool it so that it resembles flagstone (page 81).

Coloring concrete: Concrete-coloring pigments—oxides, mostly—can be used to integrally color a concrete mix. Besides a wide variety of earth colors, green and blue are available. Colors are intensified when you substitute white portland cement in the mix for regular gray. For greater economy, color only the surface layer, using plain uncolored concrete for the base. Economical dry-shake concrete coloring mixes can be purchased in several colors (page 81). Organic masonry stains are simply painted on; results are less permanent than integral coloring.

Seeding aggregate

TOOLKIT
- Stock for strikeoff
- Square shovel
- Darby, wood float, or piece of wood
- Magnesium hand float
- Hose
- Nylon broom or brush

1 ▶ Striking the concrete
Place the slab in the usual manner but strike it off about 1/2" lower than the form boards (right).

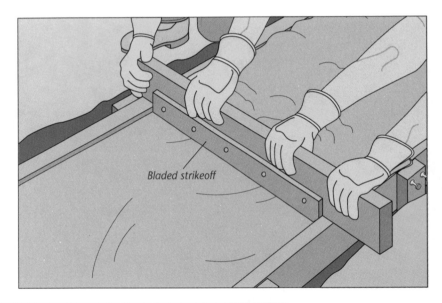

Bladed strikeoff

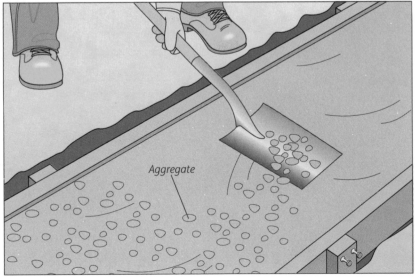

Aggregate

◀ 2 Spreading the aggregate
Soon after striking off, distribute the aggregate evenly in a single layer over the slab using a square shovel (left).

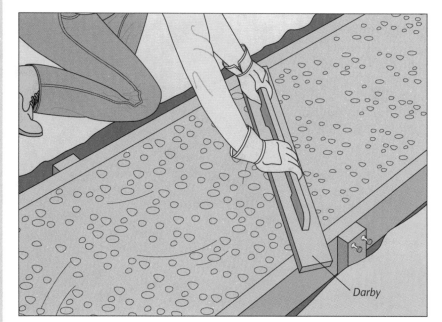

3 Floating
Using a darby, a piece of wood, or a float, press the aggregate down until it lies just below the surface of the concrete *(left)*. Then refloat the concrete with a magnesium hand float.

Darby

4 Exposing the aggregate
When the concrete has hardened to the point where it will just support your weight on knee boards without denting, you can begin exposing the aggregate. Gently broom or brush (nylon bristles are best) the concrete while wetting down the surface with a fine water spray *(right)*. Stop when the tops of the stones show, taking care not to dislodge the aggregate.

Take extra care in curing exposed aggregate surfaces; the bond to the aggregate must be strong. See page 77 for instructions on curing. Any cement haze left on the stones can be removed later on with a 10% muriatic acid solution (for more information on cleaning concrete, turn to page 88).

Nylon-bristle broom

PUTTING YOUR STAMP ON CONCRETE

Concrete stamping is an attractive option for such projects as driveways and patios; it achieves the look of unit masonry with the rapid coverage and strength of cast concrete. The advantages of concrete stamping lie in potential time and cost savings.

Concrete stamping makes a slab resemble brick, tile, adobe, or stone. The characteristic fan-shaped pattern of European cobblestone pavings is one of the most popular patterns. Several brick patterns are available; these can be left as is, in which case they resemble brick in

sand, or the stamped "joints" can be mortared so that they resemble regular brick mortar joints.

Stamping can either be done by the do-it-yourselfer or by a contractor. The technique is simple: First, a regular slab is cast and floated smooth (often the slab is colored). Then, an interlocking grid of patterned aluminum or plastic stamps is pressed into the slab. Workers stand on the grids and pound on them to force them into the concrete. A final going-over with a float fixes any blemishes, and the project is cured in the usual manner.

Using rock salt

TOOLKIT
- Wood float or piece of wood
- Magnesium hand float (optional)

Scattering the salt

Sprinkle coarse rock salt sparingly over the surface of floated concrete; embed it using a wood float or a piece of wood *(right)*. Depending upon the smoothness you desire, finish the surface by floating with a wood or magnesium hand float; the latter will produce a smoother surface. After curing the slab *(page 77)*, simply wash out the salt.

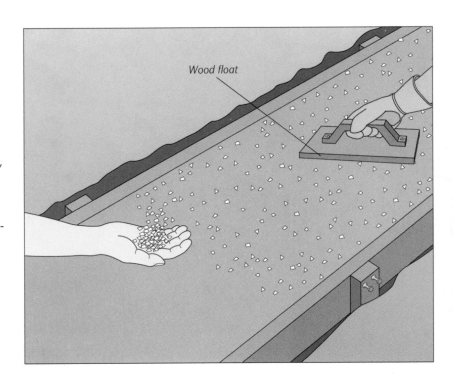

Wood float

Applying a travertine finish

TOOLKIT
- Broom (optional)
- Wallpaper or dash brush
- Steel trowel

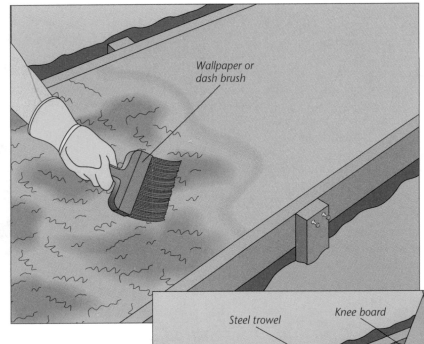

Wallpaper or dash brush

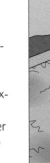

1 ▶ Brushing on mortar

After striking off, initial smoothing, and floating, roughen the surface slightly with a broom— or leave it very roughly floated. Using a large brush, dash a 1:2 cement-sand mix unevenly over the surface *(left)*. Coloring the mixture *(page 82)* to contrast with the concrete heightens the effect.

2 ▶ Troweling the mortar

When the slab can support you on knee boards, trowel the surface, knocking down the high spots *(right)*. The result is a stony texture—smooth on the high spots and rougher in the low spots. Cure the slab in the usual way *(page 77)*.

Steel trowel   Knee board

TOOLKIT
• Convex jointer
  or copper pipe
• Magnesium
  hand float
• Paintbrush
• Soft brush

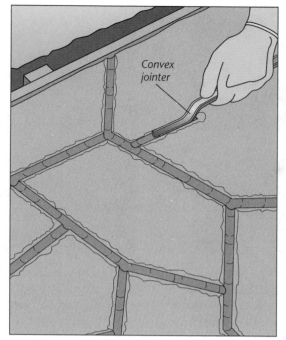

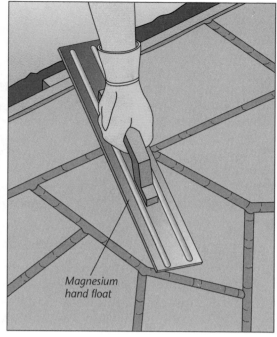

Convex jointer

Magnesium hand float

1 Tooling the surface
Tool the concrete immediately after striking off and floating. Use a convex jointer or make a bend in a short length of 1/2" to 3/4" copper pipe to make a good tool for this work. Sketch your pattern in advance and work from the plan. Erasures are awkward, so you need a sure hand.

2 Floating
When the water sheen has disappeared, do the final floating, brushing away crumbs and smoothing out blemishes with a magnesium hand float *(above)* and a paintbrush; then lightly redo the tooling. Float again for a very smooth finish. Touch up the surface with a soft brush and cure the slab.

Coloring concrete

TOOLKIT
For dusting method:
• Wood float or
  magnesium
  hand float
• Steel trowel and
  broom (optional)
For layered method:
• Stock for strikeoff
For staining:
• Paintbrush

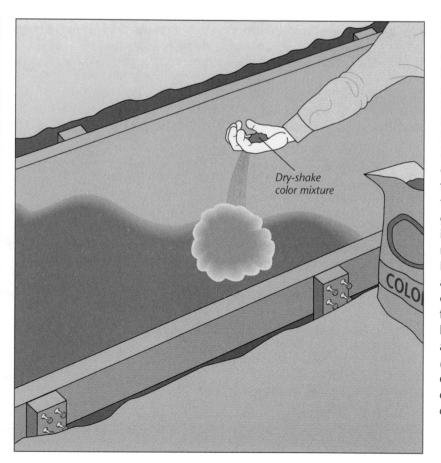

Dry-shake color mixture

COLOR

Using a coloring mixture
Check the package for how much mixture to use in each application. Dust a dry-shake coloring mixture onto a freshly floated slab *(left)*, letting the color sift evenly through your fingers. Color is easier to scatter without gloves; be sure to wash immediately and apply moisturizing lotion. Float the surface and apply a second layer of color. Finish the surface with a float, followed by a steel trowel and brooming, if desired *(page 77)*. Once floated, the mixture will color the top 1/8" to 1/4" of the slab.

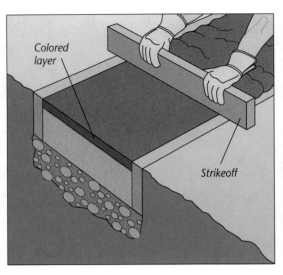

Placing colored concrete
To apply a layer of colored concrete, strike off the slab 1/2" below the top of the forms. Wait for the slab to firm up and for the water sheen to disappear. Add pigment to a small batch of cement-sand mix, and place a layer over the fresh slab, striking it off flush *(above)*. Finish and cure as usual.

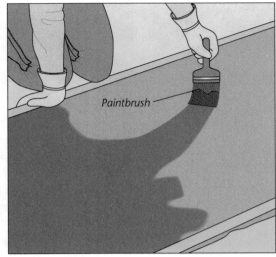

Using organic concrete stain
First finish the slab and let it cure. (Concrete to be stained should be clean and dry.) Then brush on concrete stain with a 4" paintbrush. Make sure the stain is intended for concrete, and follow the directions on the container. You'll need to restain the slab periodically.

CASTING PAVING BLOCKS

Cast-concrete paving blocks can be used for everything from pathways to patios. Laid on sand with large open joints, then filled with turf or ground cover, they quickly become a part of your garden. You can buy the units precast, but the techniques are simple, and if you make your own, you are assured of getting something distinctive that suits your project.

Three techniques are discussed here, followed by a grab bag of ideas for forms *(page 86)*. All the techniques used in finishing and texturing concrete (starting on page 78) apply to paving blocks—review them before you begin. For general information on mixing concrete, see pages 63 to 66.

The easiest way to make stepping-stones is to cast them in place in the ground, as shown below. For a more controlled edge, you can cast your paving blocks in a mold *(opposite)*. This method lends itself to smaller, lighter blocks. If you have a large area to cover, such as a long walk or a patio, a multiple-grid mold *(page 84)* will speed up the job.

Using a ground mold

TOOLKIT
• Square shovel
• Wood float or magnesium hand float

1 ▶ Digging and filling the hole

Dig a hole at least 1 1/2" deep for each "stone," contouring it as you like and keeping the sides sharply cut and fairly vertical. For easy walking, space the steps no more than 18" from the center of one to the center of the next. If you are working in a lawn, plan to keep the tops of the stones below ground level to allow for mowing.

Use the concrete mix given on page 64 to fill the holes, with a maximum 1/2" aggregate. Make sure to clean the shovel thoroughly before using it again to dig.

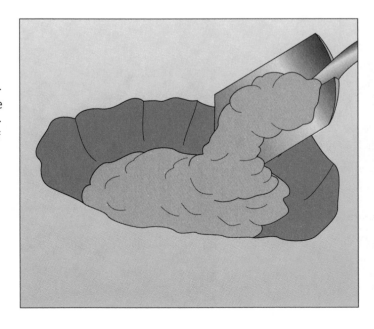

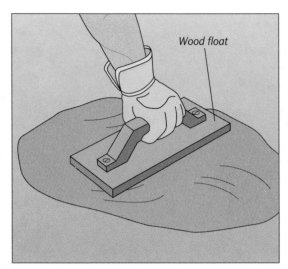

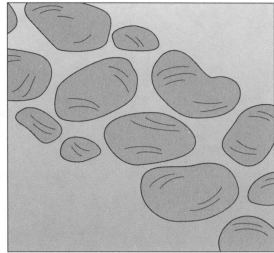

2 | Finishing the stepping-stones

Consolidate the concrete with the shovel; then finish the tops with a wood float *(above, left)* or magnesium hand float. Cover and cure the stepping-stones as described for concrete pavings on page 69. You might want to try the travertine texture *(page 80)* to enhance the look of stone. The finished pathway should have an easy natural look that resembles random stones *(above, right)*.

Using a single mold

TOOLKIT
- Saw
- Screwdriver
- Stock for strikeoff
- Square shovel
- Wood float or magnesium hand float (optional)

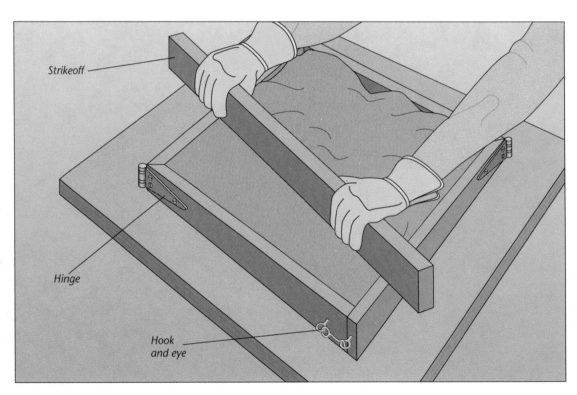

1 | Making the mold and placing the concrete

A closed mold is the easiest to make. Use 1x2 lumber or any sturdy wood. Hinge one or two corners and add a hook and eye to close the open corner, as shown. Use screws to fasten any fixed corners.

To cast the blocks, coat the mold with form-release agent and place it on a sheet of plywood or plastic, a sand bed, or other smooth surface.

Fill the box with a stiff concrete mix *(page 64)* with a maximum 1/2" aggregate. Pack in the concrete with a square shovel, and strike it off *(above)*. Placing a bottom in the box form can create interesting designs, that, when turned over, become the surface *(page 86)*. Float the surface if desired *(page 76)*, or use the block's smooth underside for the stepping surface.

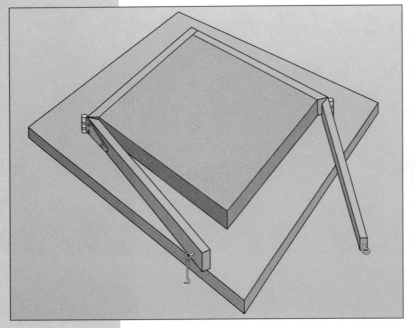

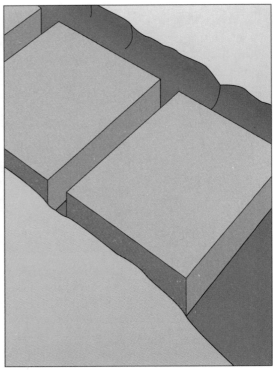

2 Unmolding the block
Wait until the concrete has set somewhat before unmolding; this won't take more than a few hours if you've used a stiff mix, and you'll be able to go right to the next block. (You'll need more than one plywood base but only one mold.) Cure the blocks just as you would a concrete slab *(page 77)*.

3 Laying the blocks
Dig a shallow trench. Place the cured blocks in the trench *(above)*, and pack earth or sand in the joints.

Using a multiple-grid mold

TOOLKIT
- Saw
- Screwdriver
- Square shovel
- Stock for strikeoff
- Wood or magnesium hand float
- Pointing trowel

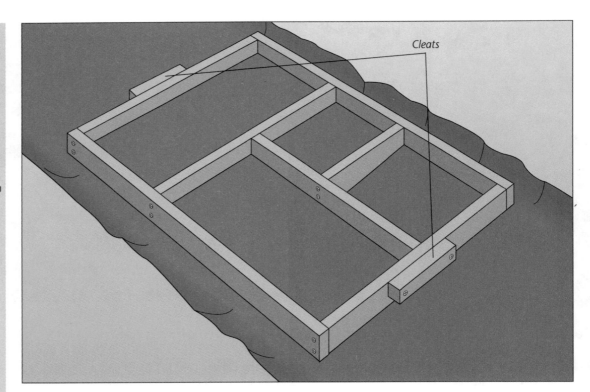

Cleats

1 Making the mold
Make the mold out of 1x2 wood, screwing the joints together. Add cleats to help lift the mold. Dig a shallow trench with a bottom of sand or gravel, or graded and well-compacted soil. Coat the mold with form-release agent, and place it in the trench.

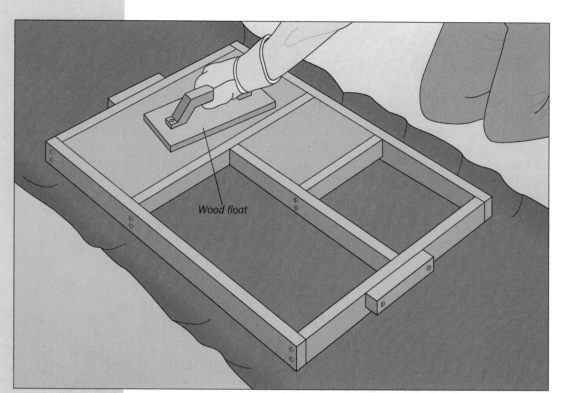

2 Casting the concrete

Fill the compartments with concrete; use the mix given on page 64 with a maximum $\frac{1}{2}$" aggregate. Consolidate the concrete with a square shovel. Strike off the form with a piece of wood and float the surface with a wood or magnesium hand float *(left)*.

Wood float

3 Lifting the mold

Remove the form as soon as the mix is stiff enough to hold its shape, by lifting it straight up. Clean up the edges of the blocks with a pointing trowel. Be sure to clean the form and recoat it with form-release agent between castings.

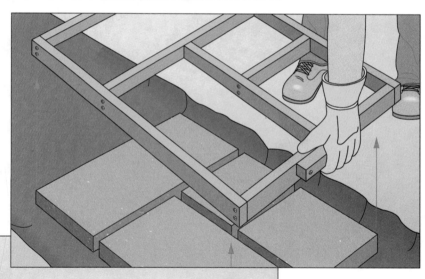

4 Finishing the path

Move the mold along and cast additional blocks as described in steps 2 and 3. Cover and cure the blocks; then, fill the joints with earth, as shown, to complete the path.

PAVING BLOCK POSSIBILITIES

Because concrete adopts the texture of the surface it's cast against, putting a bottom on a single mold and placing objects in it can create a variety of effects. You can get anything from smooth, glossy surfaces (cast against plastic sheeting or glass), to sand-blasted wood, to rubber-mat, to pebbles. One interesting surface involves laying plastic sheeting over pebbles before casting concrete on it. Turned right-side up, the casting shows an attractive dimpled look. To set you thinking, a few of the many possibilities are shown below. Materials like small stones will stick to the surface, while others, such as sand, will simply leave a surface

texture. Molds can generally be made of 1x2 wood, but if you're including material that will take from the thickness of the block, use wider lumber to maintain a minimum $1^1/_2$" thickness. Finer patterns can be brought out if you cast with $1:2^1/_4$ cement-sand mix.

All molds, especially those involving moldings and small pieces of wood, should be liberally coated with form-release agent before casting begins. It's also a good idea to press paste wax into all corners; this gives a block with rounded edges that is released easily from the mold.

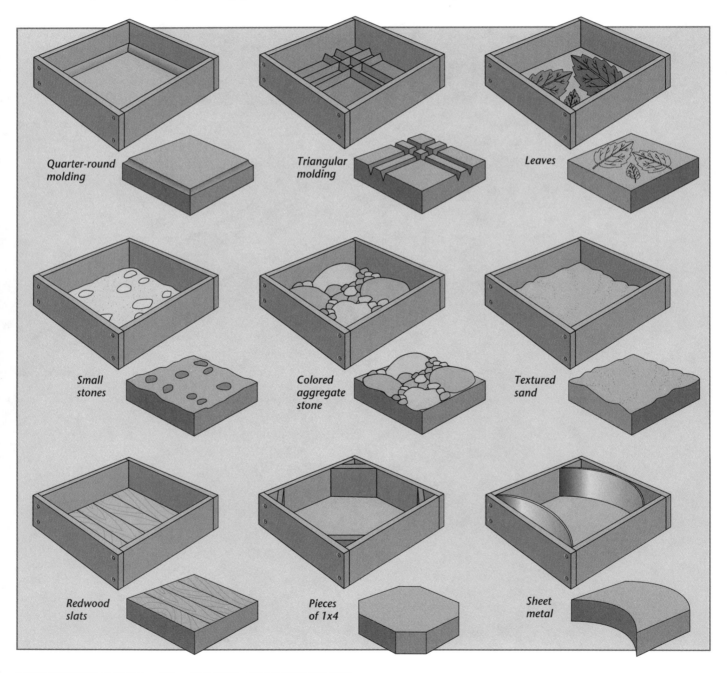

Quarter-round molding

Triangular molding

Leaves

Small stones

Colored aggregate stone

Textured sand

Redwood slats

Pieces of 1x4

Sheet metal

MAINTAINING AND REPAIRING MASONRY

Although masonry materials are fairly maintenance-free, they may require occasional cleaning, and in spite of their durability, they can be damaged. This chapter is your guide to the care and repair of masonry.

Most masonry can be kept clean with plain water, but you may occasionally have a problem with smears and stains that water can't cure. The section starting on the next page will tell you how to clean off everything from mortar smears to smoke and soot.

Cracked and broken bricks and blocks, crumbling mortar joints, and chipped and broken concrete are problems that may never occur in a well-made masonry structure. But shifting earth, impacts, and freeze-thaw cycles are beyond human control, and they can damage even a good mason's work. The section starting on page 89 guides you through the repair of brick, block, and stone structures. The section that starts on page 92 tells you how to fix damaged cast concrete, and the right way to patch stucco. In addition to some of the tools shown on page 19 and 63, you'll need a narrow-blade cold chisel for chipping away old masonry. The chisel can be tapped with a ball-peen hammer for light work such as chipping away at mortar, or with a hand-drilling hammer for heavy work, such as breaking up concrete. Remember always to wear eye protection.

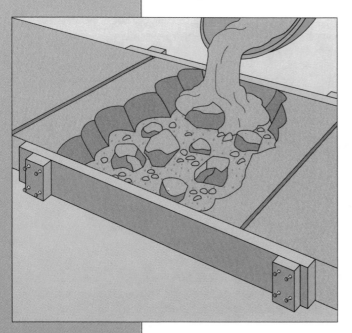

Badly damaged concrete may need to be broken up and a whole section replaced, as shown. However, as you'll learn in the section on repairing cast concrete, cracks and chipped step edges can be patched more simply.

CLEANING MASONRY

Efflorescence is a white, powdery deposit caused by water dissolving the mineral salts contained in mortar; mortar smears are an inevitable result of learning to work with masonry. Both efflorescence and mortar smears are common problems; see the information below for how to clean away these marks.

Many other substances can stain the surface of your project. For the most part, you can use ordinary household detergents, cleansers, and scouring powders. Some stains will require acid. Specific remedies for each type of stain, and some cautions, are given below.

Do not use acids on marble or limestone. Clean with water only, as even detergents can be harmful. Always use fiber brushes; steel brushes are too abrasive and may leave rust marks. Sometimes you can clean stone by rubbing it with a piece of the same type of rock.

MAINTENANCE TIP

PREVENTING STAINS
Bear in mind that anything strong enough to really stain masonry has probably penetrated the surface. Complete removal of such stains is very difficult, if not impossible, so try some preventive maintenance.

Surfaces such as a brick kitchen floor or barbecue area should be sealed thoroughly with a commercial sealer. Non-yellowing sealers with a silicone base work best. You should apply 3 or 4 coats for adequate protection.

TIPS ON CLEANING MASONRY

Efflorescence: The mineral salts that appear as efflorescence, especially on brick paving, are carried to the surface by water, which then evaporates, leaving them behind. The deposits will disappear once all the salts have been leached out, but this may take a couple of years. If you're impatient, try brushing and scrubbing the deposits away without using water; then follow with a thorough hosing. Water tends to redissolve some of the salts and they will reappear again later. Remove as much as you can by dry scrubbing before using water. In an extreme case, follow the directions for removing mortar smears.

Mortar smears: Remove these with muriatic acid, available at masonry supply stores. The acid works by attacking the calcium contained in cement and lime. Use a 1:9 acid-water solution on concrete, concrete block, and dark brick. On light-colored brick, this solution may leave stains, so use a 1:14 or 1:19 solution. Do not use acid on colored concrete; it may leach out the color. Never use it on marble or limestone. CAUTION: When preparing the solution, always pour the acid slowly into the water—never the reverse. Wear eye protection, a face shield, and rubber gloves, and work in a well-ventilated area. First wet the wall; then apply the acid with a stiff brush to a small area at a time, let it stand for 3 or 4 minutes, and flush thoroughly with water.

Muriatic acid may change the color of masonry, at least slightly; bear this in mind when cleaning large surfaces. You may want to treat the whole area to be sure to obtain an even color.

Oil and grease: Before the stain has penetrated, scatter fine sawdust, cement powder, or hydrated lime over the surface. If you catch it in time, these materials will soak up much of the oil or grease and then can be simply swept up. If the stain has penetrated, try dissolving it with a commercial degreaser or emulsifier. These are available at masonry and home supply centers and at auto suppliers; follow the manufacturer's directions. Residual stains can sometimes be lightened with household bleach, as explained for rust. Avoid hazardous solvents such as kerosene, benzene, or gasoline; they aren't worth the risks of fire or toxic inhalation.

Paint: To clean up freshly spilled paint, wipe and scrub it up with a rag soaked in the solvent specified for the paint. For dried paint, use a commercial paint remover, following the manufacturer's instructions.

Rust: Ordinary household bleach will lighten rust stains (and most others). Scrub it in, let it stand, then rinse the surface thoroughly. A stronger remedy is a pound of oxalic acid mixed into a gallon of water; follow the mixing directions for muriatic acid given for mortar smears. Brush on the acid, let it stand for 3 or 4 minutes, then hose it off. Remember that acid washes (and bleach) can affect the color of a surface. Test them in an inconspicuous area first.

Smoke and soot: Scrub with a household scouring powder and a stiff brush, then rinse with water.

REPAIRING UNIT MASONRY

Most trouble in a mortared wall or paving develops at the mortar joints. Sometimes the shrinking of mortar without lime will cause the joints to open; mortar with lime often just crumbles.

Freeze-thaw cycles worsen the problem. Water penetrates the tiniest cracks; upon freezing, it expands, enlarging the cracks and making it easier for the process to recur. Renewing the mortar joints will solve shrinking, crumbling, and cracking.

Settling of a mortared wall or paving will crack the joints, and sometimes the units themselves. A heavy impact can do the same thing. This cracking calls for replacement of the mortar and possibly one or more units; in extreme cases, a whole section may need to be completely rebuilt.

You'll find directions for all these repairs in the following pages. The information applies to all unit masonry walls and pavings (brick, block, adobe, and stone)—even though the drawings show only brick. Stone can be repaired in the same way as other units, although it may be more difficult to remove damaged units and to fit a new unit into the gap.

Renewing mortar joints

TOOLKIT
- Narrow-blade cold chisel
- Ball-peen hammer
- Paintbrush
- Joint filler or small pointing trowel
- Hawk
- Small piece of wood for tamping deep joints
- Joint-striking tool

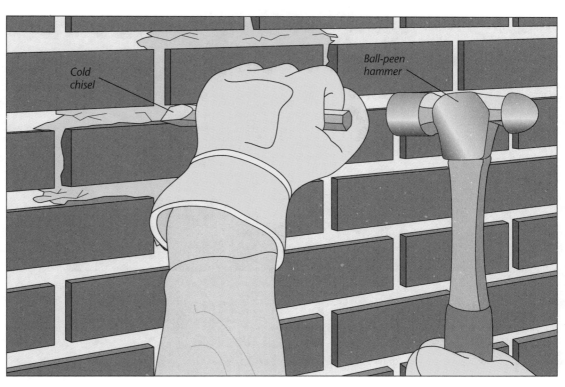

1 Chiseling out old mortar
Fresh mortar will not adhere to old. Chisel out the cracked and crumbling old mortar with a narrow-blade cold chisel and a ball-peen hammer, exposing as much of the mortar-bearing faces of the units as possible. Expose the joints to a depth of at least 3/4", then thoroughly brush and blow them out, using an old paintbrush. Always wear eye protection.

2 Mixing mortar and filling joints
Dampen the area with a brush or a fine spray of water. Mix Type N mortar *(page 20)* to a stiff consistency while waiting for the surface moisture to evaporate. (If you're repairing stone, mix mortar without lime—see page 45.) When the units are damp, but not shiny wet, use a joint filler or small pointing trowel to press mortar into the joints. You may find that a hawk will help you hold mortar close to the job.

Fill the joints completely, tamping the mortar in well (use a small piece of wood for deep joints). Masons call this "pointing." Tool the joints when the mortar is stiff enough *(page 31)*. Keep the repair damp for 4 days to cure the mortar.

Filling long cracks

TOOLKIT
• Tar paper, cardboard, or funnel for walls
OR
• Bent coffee can for paving

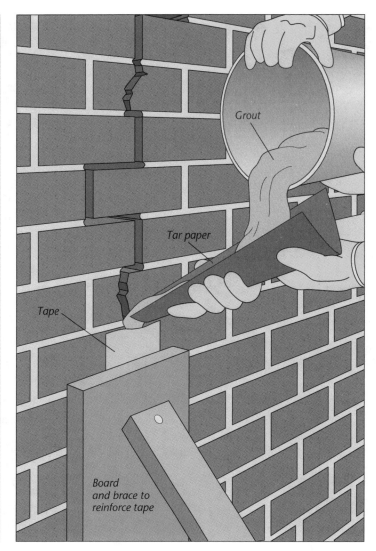

Grout

Tar paper

Tape

Board and brace to reinforce tape

Grouting

You can fix long cracks by following the directions on page 89 for renewing mortar joints, but you'll probably find grouting easier. Work with a helper if possible.

Dampen the cracked surfaces several hours before grouting. Then, when they are no longer shiny wet, pour grout *(page 20)* into vertical cracks in walls through a tar paper *(left)* or cardboard chute, or a funnel. Use wide, waterproof, surgical adhesive tape to dam up the grout in vertical cracks. If you have trouble getting the tape to adhere to the wall, hold it in place by bracing a board against it, as shown.

Fill 3' or 4' of crack at a time, waiting several hours between pours to let the grout set. Keep the area damp for 4 days to cure the grout.

Replacing an individual masonry unit

TOOLKIT
• Narrow-blade cold chisel
• Ball-peen hammer
• Brush
• Mason's trowel
• Joint-striking tool

1 Testing the unit

When a unit is badly damaged, you can replace it, but only if the unit carries no load, that is, supporting some of the weight of the wall. Check whether the unit is carrying a load by trying to move some of the broken pieces—if the pieces move, you can take the unit out and replace it with a new brick or block. If the pieces seem reluctant to move, the unit is probably carrying a load; leave it alone, or consult a professional mason before removing it.

ASK A PRO

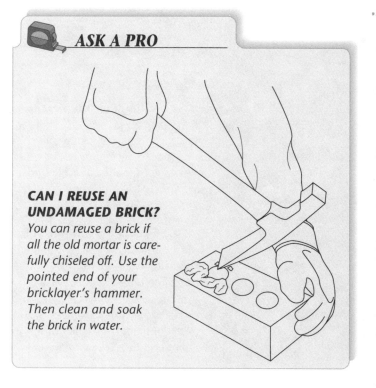

CAN I REUSE AN UNDAMAGED BRICK?
You can reuse a brick if all the old mortar is carefully chiseled off. Use the pointed end of your bricklayer's hammer. Then clean and soak the brick in water.

2 **Removing the unit**
To replace a unit, put on safety glasses and chip out the old mortar with a narrow-blade cold chisel. Work carefully so as not to disturb adjacent units. Once the mortar is out, you should be able to remove the unit. If necessary, break it up carefully with the chisel and remove the pieces. Clean up the cavity, removing all the old mortar.

Fresh mortar

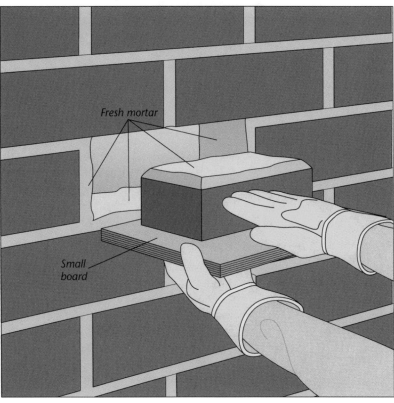

Fresh mortar

Small board

3 **Installing the new unit**
Wet the cavity and the replacement unit with a brush or fine spray of water, then prepare a batch of mortar with a 1:2 cement-sand mix (no lime) to the consistency of soft mud. (Turn to page 20 for more on mortar.) Make sure the cavity is damp but not wet. For paving, apply a thick layer of mortar to the bottom and sides of the cavity *(above, left)*; make sure the unit is level with the surrounding ones. If you're working on a wall, also apply mortar to the top of the new unit *(above, right)*. Push the new unit into place; a small board will aid in its alignment with a wall, as shown. Mortar should be squeezed from the joints; if not, add more. Trim off excess mortar and tool the joints *(page 31)*. Keep the area damp for 4 days to cure the mortar.

Rebuilding entire sections

TOOLKIT
• Cold chisel and ball-peen hammer
• Joint-striking tool

Choosing a strategy
Extensive damage calls for rebuilding. Whatever the extent of the damage, repair proceeds in the same way: work from the top down when taking damaged units out of a wall, and from the middle outward when fixing a paving. Reverse the process when you rebuild. Use a narrow-blade cold chisel to work on the mortar joints. Don't just bash away at the damaged units themselves; you may do further damage. If only a few units are damaged, replace them by following the instructions on the previous page for replacing individual units; if the damage is extensive, follow the instructions for building unit masonry walls *(page 17)*, or for unit paving *(page 49)*. Tool the joints *(page 31)* and keep the area damp for 4 days to cure the mortar.

REPAIRING CAST CONCRETE

Concrete is hard and durable; yet if it is not placed, finished, and cured correctly, flaws can develop. Impacts, shifting earth, and freeze-thaw cycles can also take their toll.

This section guides you through a range of concrete repairs: the correction of surface flaws and simple cracks, the repair of broken step edges, and the rebuilding of heavily damaged slabs. Instructions on repairing stucco, a cement-based material, conclude the section.

The security of any patch job on concrete largely depends upon the care you take in surface preparation.

Always clean all dust and debris from the area to be repaired using a scrub brush and a commercial concrete-cleaning agent, and soak it thoroughly—even the previous day—before beginning work. There should be no standing water, but surfaces must be damp to ensure a good bond.

In any repair in which the patch will be thin or will need to be feathered at its edges, you'll find the extra strength of commercial latex or epoxy-cement patching compounds (sold under various trade names) well worth their higher cost.

Correcting surface flaws

TOOLKIT
- Small sledgehammer
- Scrub brush
- Wood float
- Magnesium hand float
- Steel trowel and broom (optional)

Fixing light damage or resurfacing

Efflorescence, the appearance of white, powdery mineral salts on the surface, tends to occur naturally, and will disappear in time. To hurry it along, follow the directions for removing efflorescence given on page 88.

If a concrete slab is allowed to dry out too fast after placement or if it is finished excessively, surface flaws may develop. The most common flaws are dusting, in which the surface wears away easily; scaling, in which thin layers flake away from the surface; and crazing, in which fine networks of surface cracks appear.

To correct these problems, use one of the following methods: For light damage, clean the area and apply a 1:1 solution of linseed oil and mineral spirits. The oil will retard further damage and help protect concrete from deteriora-

tion due to the use of de-icing salts. You'll need to renew this coating every two years or so.

If the damage is bad enough to call for resurfacing, use either regular 1:2¼ portland cement-sand mix or sand mix to which a commercial latex-based bonding compound has been added, especially for thin layers.

Prepare the surface by gently removing all loose and flaking concrete using a small sledgehammer; wear eye protection. Scrub the area clean and soak it as described above.

Mix the patching material and apply it with a magnesium hand float using as little water as possible, or if using a latex-based mixture, follow the manufacturer's instructions. Finish the surface of the patch to match existing surfaces and cure it fully *(page 77)*.

Filling cracks

TOOLKIT
- Pointing trowel
- Cold chisel
- Hand-drilling hammer
- Paintbrush (optional)
- Pointing trowel
- Wood float
- Magnesium hand float or steel trowel and broom

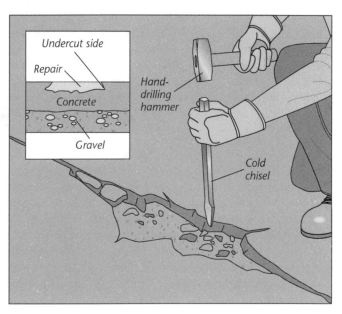

Making a patch

Fill cracks up to about ⅛" wide with a stiff paste of cement and water or a cement-based caulk. Clean out larger cracks with a cold chisel and a hand-drilling hammer *(left)*, creating a pocket ¾" deep or more. Undercut the sides *(inset)* to lock the patch. Prepare the area as described above; then fill the crack with 1:2¼ cement-sand mix with the consistency of soft mud, or a latex patching compound. To improve the bond, coat the area first with a thick mix of cement and water, the consistency of paint; scrub it in with a brush. Apply the patch immediately with a pointing trowel. Finish to match adjacent areas, cover, and cure it fully *(page 77)*.

Fixing step edges

TOOLKIT
- Cold chisel
- Hand-drilling hammer
- Scrub brush
- Paintbrush
- Mason's trowel
- Edger
- Steel trowel

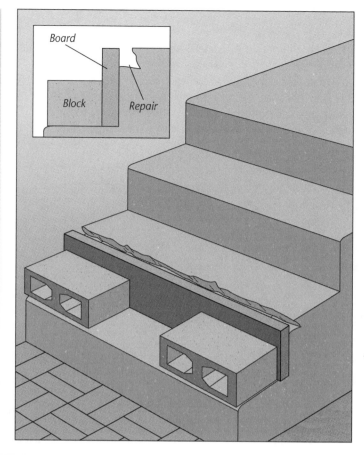

Board

Block   Repair

1 Preparing the site
Here, as in correcting surface flaws *(page 92)*, you can choose either regular cement-sand mix, or one of the commercial latex patching compounds.

If a piece has broken away from a step, simply cement it back into place using an outdoor-type epoxy adhesive (follow the manufacturer's instructions). If the damage is more extensive, chisel away the concrete (wear eye protection) until you have an undercut ledge of sound concrete that will support and retain a patch.

Premixed commercial latex patching compounds are often stiff enough to support themselves. However, if you use a regular cement-sand mix or are making large repairs, simple temporary formwork is a good idea. This can be nothing more than a board held against the step edge with blocks, as shown.

Thoroughly clean and then dampen the area several hours before placing the patch.

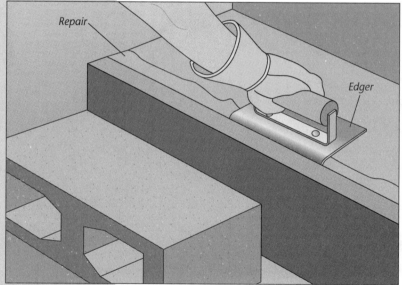

Repair

Edger

Steel trowel   Finished edge

2 Patching
Begin by brushing on a coat of thick cement-and-water mixture, the consistency of paint, or a commercial latex bonding compound, using a paintbrush. Follow it immediately with either a 1:2$\frac{1}{4}$ cement-sand mix made as dry as possible or a commercial latex patching compound. Thoroughly prod the material with a trowel to eliminate air pockets, then smooth it with the same trowel or a steel trowel. When the patch has stiffened slightly, finish it with an edger *(above)*.

3 Finishing the repair
Carefully remove the form board and use a steel trowel to touch up the face of the step *(above)*. Cover and cure the patch for several days *(page 77)* or, if you're using a commercial compound, follow the manufacturer's instructions.

Mending a heavily damaged slab

TOOLKIT
- Sledgehammer
- Scrub brush

1 Breaking up the slab

Badly broken concrete slabs should be rebuilt with more concrete. If the damage is extensive, this may mean erecting forms and casting a new slab. Wearing safety goggles, begin by breaking up the damaged area with a sledgehammer, saving the pieces to use as filler in the repair.

If the gravel base has sunk, build it up with more gravel and bits of broken concrete. Clean the edges of the patch area and saturate everything with water. Wait several hours for the standing water to be absorbed before placing the fresh concrete. If the broken area extends to an edge, erect temporary forms, as shown below.

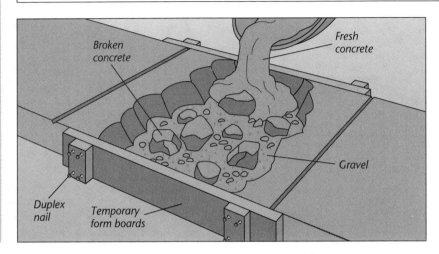

2 Placing the concrete

Mix a batch of $1:2^1/4:2^1/2$ cement-sand-aggregate concrete sufficient to fill the area. Refer to page 63 for information on buying and mixing concrete. Put some of the broken pieces back as filler. Place, finish, and cure the new concrete according to the directions found on page 73.

Patching stucco

TOOLKIT
- Cold chisel and hand-drilling hammer, or putty knife
- Scrub brush
- Mason's trowel or putty knife
- Wood float, sponge, or piece of carpet (optional)

1 Preparing the area

You can repair damage to stucco walls with 1:3 cement-sand mortar to which a maximum of $1/10$ part hydrated lime has been added; for small jobs, a commercial stucco-patching compound is the most convenient and economical.

Wearing eye protection, remove all damaged material with a cold chisel or a putty knife until you get down to a bed of sound stucco. If you get down to the lath or stucco netting underlying the stucco (*right*), plan to make the repair in two layers.

Scrub the area and moisten it with a brush or a fine spray of water.

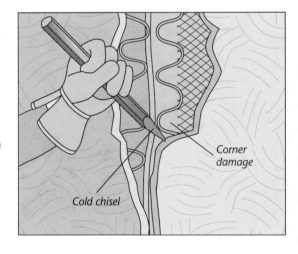

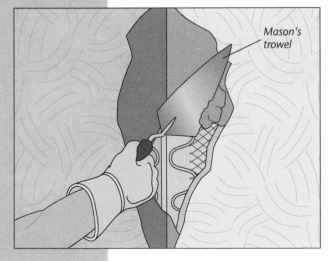

2 Patching

Mix the mortar or patching compound to a workable but not runny consistency. (If the wall is to be painted, use regular gray cement in the mortar. If the color is integral, see your supplier for coloring oxides, and use white cement and sand in the mortar mix.) Apply the patch with a mason's trowel or putty knife, smoothing or texturing to match the original surface. Textured surfaces can be produced with a wood float, a sponge, or a piece of carpet.

To cure the repair, keep it moist for 4 days by misting it with water. If it's windy or hot, or if the area is in strong sunlight, cover the patch with plastic sheeting or burlap (keep damp) to help retain moisture. If you're applying two layers, cure the first for at least 2 days before adding the second.

MASONRY GLOSSARY

Aggregate
A basic ingredient in concrete; acts as a filler and helps control shrinkage. Gravel or crushed stone are coarse aggregate; sand is referred to as fine aggregate.

Air-entraining agent
Added to concrete to make it more reisistant to freeze-thaw damage. Also makes it more workable.

Ashlar stone
Square-cut stone that is laid in courses like brick.

Backfill
Earth that has been dug out from one spot and filled into another. Does not offer the uniform support of earth that has been undisturbed.

Batter
The inward slope of a stone wall; ensures that the stones are held in place by resting against each other.

Bed
A layer of mortar or sand on which masonry units are laid.

Bed joint
A horizontal joint in a masonry wall.

Bond
The method by which units are interlocked, the pattern made by units on the face of a wall, and the adhesion of mortar to units.

Bond beam
A course of concrete blocks from which the webs have been removed. This course is then grouted, reinforcing the wall.

Bond stone
A large stone that extends the thickness of a stone wall, tying the wythes together.

Buttering
The act of spreading mortar on the edge or end of a masonry unit using the tip of the trowel.

Cast concrete
Concrete that is placed in a form or mold and allowed to harden, as opposed to prefabricated concrete block. Sometimes referred to as "poured concrete."

Cement, portland
A manufactured product, as opposed to natural cement. A basic ingredient in both mortar and concrete. Ingredients include lime, silica, alumina, and iron.

Closer brick
The last brick inserted in a course, either whole or cut.

Closure block
The last block inserted in a course.

Closure brick
A cut brick used to fill in an odd-sized spot in a course to continue a bond pattern.

Compression
Crushing pressure; masonry has high compressive strength.

Concrete
A building material composed of portland cement, water, sand, and coarse aggregate. The mixture hardens as the water combines chemically with the cement.

Control joint
A joint formed in a concrete slab as a hidden spot for the slab to crack. Also, an unmortared, continuous vertical joint in long brick and block walls that allows the sections to move independently.

Course
A single layer of masonry units. "Front" refers to the course along the most visible face of the wall, and "backup" to the one behind it. "Course" can also refer to both rows together.

Curing
The act of keeping mortar, grout, or concrete moist for several days while it hardens, to help the cement and water react more completely.

Duplex nail
A double-headed nail used for temporary form work. First head is driven against the work; second head is used to pull the nail out.

Face shell
The outside edges of a concrete block; exposed when laid in the wall.

Floating
The act of smoothing the surface of plastic concrete with a flat tool, called a float.

Footing
An underground concrete slab that supports a masonry wall.

Form
A wooden frame built to contain cast concrete while it hardens.

Form-release agent
A product used to coat forms before concrete is placed. Allows the form to be separated from the concrete. Can be either oil- or silicone-based.

Grading
The act of digging out an area to be paved to the desired level, and sloped to allow for drainage.

Grout
A thin, pourable cement-sand-water mixture. Used to fill concrete block cores, or to fill between wythes of a brick wall to secure steel reinforcing. Grout is also used to fill joints between tiles, and to repair cracks in masonry.

Header
A brick laid flat, running across the thickness of a wall. Used in some bond patterns to tie the wythes together.

Head joint
A vertical joint in a unit masonry wall.

Isolation joint
Material added to allow independent movement where a new concrete slab adjoins existing concrete.

Knee boards
Boards used to distribute weight while kneeling to finish concrete. The boards rest on the forms.

Lead
A set of partial courses at either end of a wall that establishes alignment. Each course is shorter than the previous one, creating a stepped shape.

Level
Exactly horizontal.

Modular sizes
Dimensions of a masonry unit that includes a mortar joint; actual size is smaller. Bricks can be bought modular or non-modular; blocks are always modular.

Mortar
The "glue" used to bond masonry units together. Typically composed of water, lime, portland cement, and sand. Mortar can also be made without lime, sometimes referred to as a cement-sand mixture. "Stiff" mortar contains very little water.

Plastic concrete
Fresh concrete that has not yet hardened. Also called "wet" concrete.

Plumb
Exactly vertical.

Raking
The act of scraping some of the mortar out of the joints to create a recess that accentuates the play of light and shadow.

Rowlock
A brick placed on edge, running the thickness of a wall. Commonly used as a wall's top course, or cap.

Rowlock stretcher
A brick placed on edge, running along the length of a wall.

Rubble stone
Rounded, uncut stone; laid without courses.

Sailor
A brick standing on end with the wide face showing.

Soldier
A brick on end with the narrow edge showing.

Stretcher
A brick lying flat, running along the length of a wall.

Striking
The act of compacting and shaping a joint with a trowel or joint-striking tool.

Striking off
The act of leveling a sand or mortar bed, or freshly-placed concrete, by dragging a strikeoff across the top. A regular strike-off is simply a board that levels the material flush with the form or edging; a bladed strikeoff levels the material below the form or edging.

Tags
Rough bits of mortar that are removed with a trowel after striking the joints.

Tamp
To compact sand, gravel, or soil using a tamper.

Tension
The stretching force that snaps a horizontal object. Adding steel reinforcement improves the tensile strength of masonry.

Throwing a mortar line
The act of placing a bed of mortar using a trowel.

Tooling
Another term for striking mortar joints.

Wall, freestanding
A wall that is not a retaining wall.

Wall, loadbearing
A wall that must support more than its own weight. Walls shown in this book are non-loadbearing.

Wall, retaining
A wall that holds back earth that is higher on one side than the other.

Wythe
A vertical set of courses, one unit thick. Brick walls shown in this book have two wythes.

INDEX